secrets of
Corvette
Detailing
SECOND EDITION

engine, chassis, interior, exterior & long-term care

MIKE ANTONICK

This second edition published in 1999 by Michael Bruce Associates, Inc., P. O. Box 396, Powell, Ohio, 43065.

© Michael B. Antonick, 1999

Unless otherwise credited, all photos are by Mike Antonick.

Cover photography by Mike Antonick.

Cover Corvette convertible, the third 1963 model built, is owned by Brian Richardson.

Wholesale: This book and others are available at discounts when ten or more books are ordered. Contact the publisher, Michael Bruce Associates, Inc., P. O. Box 396, Powell, Ohio 43065.

Trade: Book stores and libraries, please contact the trade distributor, MBI Publishing, 729 Prospect Avenue, P. O. Box 1, Osceola, WI 54020-0001.

Printed and bound in the United States of America.

Contents

Chapter 1

First things first

There are many books dedicated to detailing automobiles, but Corvette is the only marque I know of that has one written specifically for it. What is it about Corvettes that justifies this? The best way to answer this is to start by citing a short chronology of *Secrets of Corvette Detailing*, second edition.

Back in 1981, Tom Warth, the founder and then president of a company called Classic Motorbooks, asked me to come up with a small auto detailing book. Tom wanted his company to sell the book, but also to give it away to his retail mail-order customers who placed orders of $50 or more. Tom had two requirements...that the book's content apply to any car, and that it be moderately priced. The finished product, *Secrets of the Show Cars*, was pocket-sized and cost $6.95. That he built Motorbooks from an operation in his basement to the largest automobile literature dealer in the world tells something of Tom's marketing prowess. He was simply the best in his field, and *Secrets of the Show Cars* was a terrific hit.

Because of my own background, *Secrets of the Show Cars* had a Corvette on its cover, and Corvettes appeared in many of the photos inside. But because of the intended market, the content had to be generalized. A few years later, it dawned on me that a new, larger *Secrets* book was needed, one that zeroed in on Corvettes. That's the genesis of the original *Secrets of Corvette Detailing*, published in 1988, now followed by this larger, expanded second edition.

So why a separate detailing book for Corvettes in the first place? We all know that some Corvette components such as knock-off and bolt-on aluminum road wheels, teakwood steering wheels, transparent lift-off roof panels, and side exhausts are not common fare for other marques. And, of course, Corvette bodies have always been fiberglass or another type of plastic composite. But isn't paint just paint, regardless of the surface to

A new, larger *Secrets* book was needed, one that zeroed in on Corvettes.

Above: In 1953, Corvette production started in a temporary facility in the customer delivery garage, an old building on Van Slyke Avenue in Flint, Michigan. Starting with the first year's production of 300, Corvette was unique to General Motors and to the automotive world. After a shaky start, European-racer-turned-Chevrolet-engineer Zora Arkus-Duntov gave the Corvette record-setting performance credentials. From production methods to its composite plastic body, nothing but nothing has ever been quite like the Corvette. For reasons uncertain, but most likely relating to early camaraderie born of clubs and meets, or as a reflex to the brutalization of Corvettes by some early owners, Corvette enthusiasts have elevated the concept of factory originality above that of any other marque's ownership group. Chevrolet photo

which it's applied? And carpet is carpet, chrome is chrome, and glass is glass. So what if it all happens to be assembled into something called Corvette?

Attitude Adjustment

Put me under oath, and I'll confess that Corvettes do share much in the way of raw materials and component parts with other cars. Heck, a year after the Corvette's fifth generation arrived in 1997, Camaro had a pretty close version of Corvette's new LS1 aluminum-block motor. The Corvette has usually been GM's technology leader, particularly in the high-performance segment. Innovations do filter down from it to other cars. And it is true that if you've mastered a technique for polishing paint, chances are it will work fine for a Corvette. But this all misses the point.

Corvettes are different. What I loved about my first, a 1963 convertible, and every one since is that nothing, but nothing, is a Corvette. I'll admit that I also like, own, and drive other cars. I've spent time in Japan and Europe and admire much about some of their products. Yet among the world's automobiles, Corvette stands alone. It is its own segment. It started with the first 1953 models. Granted, those first Corvettes were far from perfect, but what an incredibly bold vehicle for its era! Think of what lumbered along our roadways in 1953. And a car like Corvette from General Motors? It amazes me to this day.

With respect to detailing, the differences in the vehicle are not as important as the attitudes of Corvette owners. What they consider original, correct, and proper for their Corvettes is a world apart from that of other marques' owners. This is not meant as a knock on other vehicles or the people who drive them. It's just the way it is, and it's why a different

Below and Left: Chevrolet introduced the Corvette to the public at its January 1953 Motorama held in New York City. Celebrities were thought to enhance the new car's panache and the photo below had Dinah Shore behind the wheel and actor George Montgomery riding shotgun. Over the years, as Corvette developed into a high performance sportscar, this approach changed. Prior to the introduction of the 1997 model, for example, magazine writers and other media were invited to sample the all-new Corvette on country roads in central Kentucky, and at Road Atlanta racecourse, shown at left. Motorama photo courtesy of Chevrolet

approach to detailing Corvettes is a fact of life. You can and should apply many of this book's detailing techniques to other cars. Some tips in *Secrets of the Show Cars* are repeated here. But you need to be careful about applying general detailing techniques to Corvettes, because those techniques may be very inappropriate.

Perhaps the best way to understand this difference in approach is to examine the word *detailing*. It implies an attention to detail. That's good. It also makes you think of the detailing shops where the affluent take their leased yuppiemobiles for periodic sprucing because their time is too valuable to consider detailing by themselves, but a shiny car is a must. Worse, it may make you think of quick-and-cheap used-car-lot detailing.

In the first edition of this book, I was quite harsh in my comments toward detailing shops. Generalizations are dangerous because there are always exceptions. Over the past decade, I've found some professional detailers who are very skilled...so skilled that I wouldn't hesitate to use their services. Even if, like me, you enjoy hands-on detailing as part of the Corvette ownership experience, there are instances where I'll recommend you seek a professional detailer rather than buy materials and learn the techniques for solving a problem you might face only once.

Now, with that disclaimer made, I'll tell about you detailing shop shortcomings. First, patrons of detailing shops think short term. They want their vehicles to look good this weekend. Long term, at most, means three years out to the end of their leases. I like Corvette thinking because it tends to be much longer term. Our country could use more of that. A Corvette enthusiast's heart pounds at the sight of a 1967 with factory-original paint. If that 1967 had visited a detailing shop every three months for a power buff, the paint would have been ground off the fender peaks around 1971. Even owners of new Corvettes who aren't planning long-term ownership cringe at the thought of exposing their Corvettes' paint to a detailing shop's power buffer every few months. Adding insult to injury, it's usually the youngest employee on the detailing shop's totem pole, the guy with the least experience, who gets assigned the buffer. Ouch!

It doesn't stop with paint. A detailing shop's engine compartment procedure often starts with a high-pressure steam cleaning. This powerful technique blasts away original stenciled codes and markings, and floats labels and decals right down the floor drain. Anybody can strip-clean an engine compartment and spray-bomb it real pretty-like with clear lacquer. Ugh. Shops that do inexpensive detailing for used-car lots are the worst in this area, and I've passed on more than one car that has had this awful treatment. In the Corvette world, this simply won't do. My cohorts and I will show you how to detail without demolishing.

Corvette philosophy is different because of its strict interpretation of originality. More on this in a moment. Merely reading this tells me that you already know that Corvette detailing demands are different from those of other cars. More knowledge is what you seek. You may want to maintain your new or nearly new Corvette in its present condition. You may want to refurbish or restore your Corvette and then keep it pristine. You know where you want to be, but not all the steps to take you there.

The words "show," "street," and "sale" appeared in the subtitle for the first edition of *Secrets of Corvette Detailing*. Those three terms describe why most Corvettes are detailed. The most common and least vigorous detailing is for street use. Street use implies that the Corvette is returning to normal use, so such things as gravel in the tire treads and a little dust don't matter. Detailing for resale isn't much different, but it could be a little more extensive if you have the luxury of restricting the Corvette's use prior to sale. Show, or concours, is the ultimate preparation level. However, even it varies within the Corvette hobby.

The intent of this text is not to provide a guidebook for success on the show circuit, although concours Corvette preparation is a fascinating subject and will be explored. No one attends a Corvette concours without wondering how certain effects were achieved. Some figure it's lots of sweat and perseverance with no great skill. Hands-on experience is key, but skill and a knowledge of the techniques are important aspects of a successful Corvette presentation. The importance of knowing what to do and how to do it can't be overstated. When you get right down to it, many owners simply don't know how to properly wash a Corvette, let alone how to refurbish, maintain, and preserve it. Just doing something a few hundred

> # Corvette detailing philosophy is different because of its strict interpretation of originality.

Pages 8 and 9: Quality shows (Corvettes at Carlisle featured here) offer enthusiasts unique insights into concours detailing and much more. Corvettes of every model and condition, parts of all descriptions, and new friendships forged, all combine to infuse a sensory overload of Corvette knowledge in a single weekend.

times doesn't mean it's being done properly.

The previous conclusion about washing skill can easily be misunderstood. It's true, but it sounds pompous. No one knows it all. Two owners could take entirely different paths to attain equally superb results. The enthusiasts I asked to be consultants for *Secrets of Corvette Detailing* know what they're doing. Their techniques and the products they use work. But this stuff isn't written in stone. Others use different techniques and products to obtain equal, perhaps better, results. Like any science, that of car care improves and changes with the discovery of new ways to do things and with new products. Just because something's new, however, doesn't mean it's better.

This all leads to the very reason I felt it necessary to rewrite *Secrets of Corvette Detailing* and to release it in the form of this new second edition. I, and the people who contributed to this book, have learned some new things. On a personal note, I've got a new favorite wax, actually a complete new waxing system. I recently bought a 1966 Corvette convertible with original, but dreadful, paint. It was dulled by years of California sun, chipped by stones, and had door dings, yet I watched a pro bring it back. I'll tell you how he did it. Since I've always changed my engine oil fairly frequently, I once considered the extra cost of synthetic oil a waste. No longer. In an expanded section on long-term care, I'll explain why Corvettes now come with Mobil 1 synthetic right from the factory and when you should, and should not, use it in your own Corvette. I'll explain why I no longer use silicone brake fluid, a reversal of my advice in this book's first edition.

The goals of Corvette restoration and preservation continue to change. An awareness of the significance of originality started spreading into the Corvette hobby in the early 1970s, but the definition of originality has evolved. Under the hood, originality once meant having the correct components, but detailing those components reached a level far exceeding

Just because something is new, however, doesn't mean it's better.

Left and above: The barcoded paper label with "ZYC" designates a 1997 Corvette engine with manual transmission. It's this type of perishable identification that Corvette enthusiasts seek to preserve by gentle cleaning during detailing. **Bottom:** Chevrolet relocated the Corvette's transmission to the rear for the redesigned 1997 model and the new layout is being studied here in a salvage specialist's area at the Corvettes at Carlisle annual show.

Above and right: Few things are more uncomfortable than sandblasting or glass beading in the open air, but a self-contained cabinet makes stripping smaller parts a breeze. Parts as large as a wheel can be top loaded into this model's glass lid. The blasting nozzle is controlled through the sealed arm slots. This type of destructive cleaning is reserved for parts that will not respond to gentler methods.

Every Corvette is genuinely factory original for but a brief moment in its life.

anything that ever left the Corvette factories at Flint, St. Louis, or Bowling Green. By the late 1980s, the factory look had been taken to the point where fresh restorations intentionally looked a little ragged in order to mimic factory sloppiness. Today, the pendulum has swung back and a slightly more polished look is preferred. Personally, I try to duplicate what the factory did on a reasonably good day, but overrestoration is still just that.

The words "factory original" will appear many times in this book. Think of what these words really mean. Factory original is the condition of a Corvette after completion at the assembly plant, but before shipment to dealers. It's not the same as "showroom" condition, because dealers prep Corvettes differently. It's not the same as "like new" because that isn't precise enough. Obviously, every Corvette is genuinely factory original for but a brief moment in its life. Returning a Corvette's condition as close as possible to that brief moment is the goal of Corvette purists.

An important point is being made here. Corvette novices make the mistake of thinking they will enhance the value of their Corvettes by stripping them and starting over. Take the engine compartment example again...a novice is tempted to remove the finishes from the metal parts and then repaint, polish, or replate everything. It looks nice, sure, but in the eyes of a Corvette collector, the value has gone south. The process of "cleaning" removed much of the Corvette's history, identity, and authenticity forever.

Many years ago, a Corvette detailing book might have advised you to start in the engine compartment with a steam cleaning, and then to attack what the steam cleaner couldn't remove with sandblasting, glass beading, or lacquer thinner. A non-Corvette detailing book written today will tell you the same thing. Today, the strip-it-and-start-over idea is wrong for Corvettes, certainly as the first step anyway. Think of it like this. Ship a rough Corvette to some fine Russian craftsmen in Siberia who have no reference material and have never laid eyes on a Corvette, and they could still make it look beautiful. Now, how much more valuable would that Corvette be if it had been left alone with its original decals and markings in place, or if it had been restored properly by enthusiasts with the experience to know precisely how Chevrolet built those cars?

I realize that anything can be taken to extremes, so let's not go off the deep end here. Remember that 1966 convertible I just mentioned with the lousy paint? I spent more money salvaging the original paint than I would have on a fresh paint job. But to me, that was money well spent. How many mostly-original-paint 1966 Corvettes are left? But after purchasing the car, a crankshaft bearing failed. Due to age and miles and long storage periods, I knew I'd have to rebuild the engine eventually, but the bearing forced the issue sooner rather than later. I suppose it would have been possible to just do a minimal repair and leave the original finish on the exterior of the engine, but it wasn't practical. When an engine is out and taken apart, this is the time to strip and clean everything, then replace any component worn beyond original specs. This car had its original engine. Properly rebuilt and maintained, it will last almost forever.

Even without a complete engine rebuild, there are times when steam cleaning and strong solvents have their place. The rule to follow for state-of-the-art Corvette care is to use the least damaging cleaner or solvent necessary to accomplish the task. There will be times when a surface will have to be reduced to its virgin state by whatever harsh means are necessary. The cadmium plating on many engine compartment components in my 1966, for example, was simply gone. So these parts were replated. It's a judgment call. Refinish if necessary, but only as a last resort. Remember, original is genuinely original just once.

The Consultants

Even if the detailing techniques outlined in these pages can be applied to other cars, this is a Corvette book. The photos depict Corvettes, and Corvette enthusiasts provided most of the nitty-gritty detailing expertise. I am most indebted to Dave Burroughs, who helped both in writing this text and in staging several photos. Additional technical help came from Pat Baker, Gordon Killebrew, Brian Hardy, Bill Munzer, Don Williams, John Amgwert, Milt Antonick, Tom Tucker and Andy Roderick.

The credentials of these men are impressive. Dave Burroughs is an aviation enthusiast who also has a passion for "midyear" Corvettes, those built between 1963 and 1967. Dave began his teen summers working at a small airport in Illinois, mowing grass and generally poking around aircraft for $50 and an hour's free flying time each week. After formal maintenance and flight training, he spent five years as a professional pilot.

Airplane people are a fussy lot. Good thing, because there isn't much room for error. Dave carried along these traits when he entered the Corvette show-car circuit. In 1976, his silver 1967 Corvette became the first Corvette to win the "triple crown," with class wins at what were then the big three Corvette shows: Bloomington in Illinois, McDorman's in Ohio, and the National Council of Corvette Clubs' national meet, held that year in Orlando, Florida.

In 1978, Dave conceived and organized the National Corvette Certification Board for judging Corvettes at the annual Bloomington

State-of-the-art Corvette care means using the least damaging cleaner or solvent.

Right: Dave Burroughs' 4000-hour restoration of a 1965 Corvette convertible with the 396 "big block" engine was the basis for hardbound and softbound editions of this book.

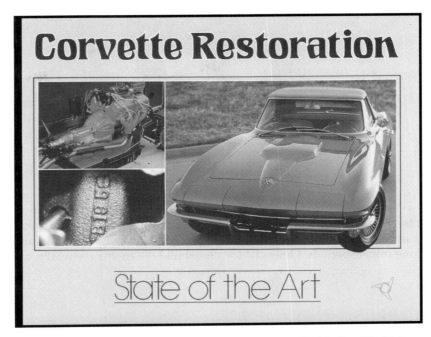

Corvette show. When you see "Bloomington Gold Certified" in a Corvette's description, you know it has met stringent criteria for originality. Dave later completed a 4,000-hour, three-year restoration of a 1965 Corvette that became the basis for hardbound and softbound editions of the book *Corvette Restoration: State of the Art.* Dave later restored two spectacular 1967 Corvettes, both with the L88 engine option. Just twenty 1967 L88s were built. The two Dave restored were an original-engine convertible and a coupe with 14 original miles on the odometer! After two decades of Corvette intensity, Dave has reverted to his first love, airplanes. He flies a Stearman and is restoring another. But his reexposure to airplanes has turned up new detailing products that work great for Corvettes, too. I'll tell you about them later.

Pat Baker is the owner of Corvette Corner, a full-line Corvette sales and service facility in Columbus, Ohio. Pat has been around Corvettes for four decades and has viewed the evolution of the hobby from every angle. He's been active on the Corvette show circuit himself, and his company handles virtually every kind of Corvette part and service except heavy collision work. Pat and his employees detail cars for customers and for their own showroom.

Gordon Killebrew retired from Corvette's Bowling Green assembly plant in 1993 after thirty years of service with General Motors. His involvement with Corvette production started in 1980, and in 1988 he joined the "action center" at Bowling Green, a now defunct (to the dismay of many) department set up to answer questions from dealers and owners. Gordon has written numerous Corvette books, and conducts Corvette repair seminars in facilities on his property in Cross Plains, Tennessee.

Brian Hardy practically grew up at the Bob McDorman Chevrolet dealership in Canal Winchester, Ohio, where his dad was the parts department manager. From lot boy during his high school years, Brian moved up through the ranks to new-car sales manager at the age of twenty-six. In addition to playing a key role in the management and operation of many of the annual McDorman Corvette shows, Brian enters his own Corvettes in concours events. He owns stock 1972, 1976, and 1985 models and a 1989 Challenge Corvette.

Above and left: The National Corvette Restorers Society (NCRS) was formed in 1974 and has always encouraged its membership to strive for genuine factory originality. The NCRS has a major annual meet which changes locations, plus regional meets at fixed locations, including a show within a show at Corvettes at Carlisle, shown here. Having a Corvette judged by the NCRS or merely viewing a Corvette prepared to NCRS standards is an excellent guide to correct underhood finishes and other detailing criteria.

John was one of the original founders of the National Corvette Restorers Society in 1974.

Bill Munzer and Don Williams have a tremendous amount of Corvette concours experience. Bill is a master of chassis, engine, and interior work, while Don is an artist in exterior body repair, refinishing, and detailing. The two men have pooled their talents to create breathtaking and successful show Corvettes that have earned more awards than Bill and Don can keep track of, and thousands of dollars in prize money. One of their joint show projects, a 1963 fuel-injected Corvette, won them a brand-new Corvette at the McDorman Corvette show in 1976. Don painted and helped restore the 1980 McDorman show winner, a 1964 Corvette owned by Frank and Sherry LaVinia. In 1981, Don teamed with Bill Munzer again to win McDorman's Best of Show title with another 1963 coupe. Don was back at McDorman's in 1987, having painted and helped to detail the show winner again—a 1965 convertible owned by Neil McBride. Both Bill and Don are nearing retirement in their day jobs and plan to join talents again by starting a Corvette restoration and detailing shop.

John Amgwert was one of the original seven founders of the National Corvette Restorers Society in 1974. From then until 1999, he was the editor of *The Corvette Restorer*, the NCRS's award-winning quarterly magazine. He has written restoration articles for *Hot Rod* and *Corvette News* and has participated in countless concours events as judge, entrant, and organizer.

Milt Antonick is my older brother by nine years, and I grew up in awe of his automobile talents. He's now an industrial designer in Detroit's auto industry. His first job in automobile design was with Studebaker, and he signed on shortly before the Avanti project got under way. He was one of two internal designers assigned to Avanti and did many of the interior renderings. Later, while at Chrysler, he headed design groups responsible for such marketing successes as the Duster, Roadrunner, and second-generation Barracuda. He financed his education by winning the top national award in GM's Fisher Body Craftsman's Guild contest for auto design and construction. Milt loves all sorts of cars and offers not only his personal expertise, but also that gleaned from the modeling shops of big Detroit automakers and small independent design studios.

Tom Tucker owns a nice little body shop set in a clump of beautiful pine trees within view of his home in Utica, Ohio. Tom has been in the auto body repair business all his adult life, and I've never known anyone better with a spray gun. Over the years he's seen every kind of paint problem and solution. More than that, Tom is an enthusiast and does all his own detailing. He goes to Hershey every year and owns several classic Chevys. The special occasion family car is a 1987 Corvette, purchased new, that sees about 400 miles per year.

Andy Roderick's garage was one of ten selected by *Car & Driver* for a "ten best" issue. *Corvette Quarterly*'s editor, Wes Raynal, came across that article and noted that Andy's garage was stuffed full of Corvettes. Wes asked me to go meet this guy and write a little something for *Corvette Quarterly*'s "I drive a Corvette" feature. Andy has a car lover's dream garage, including tiled floor and lift, and his 1998 convertible was as meticulously detailed as any street-driven Corvette I'd ever seen. So once the interview was out of the way, I shifted into detailing-secrets mode and found out how Andy keeps his cars looking so beautiful.

There are many other people from whom these men and I have learned, or who have volunteered tips and suggestions. They include Kent Brooks, Steve Dangremond, Bob Dienes, Don Ellefsen, the late Sam Folz, Cliff Gottlob, Mike Hansen, Paul Kitchen, Jim Krughoff, Gary Lisk, Bill Locke, Dr. Bill Miller, Chip Miller, Bill Mock, Errol McKoy, Jim Prather, Captain

Top: *This portable air tank, equipped with a burst nozzle, is a great way to blow away dust, or to dry small parts.*
Left: *Here's a Corvette concours entrant's trunk of tricks. Touch-up paint, silicone, solvents, cleaners, polish, wax, brushes...it's all here.*

L. W. Reimer, Jr., Sal Ricotta, Dale Smith, Steve Ward, and Jerry Weichers.

Concours experts are often reluctant to reveal their secrets, not because they don't want others to know how they do these things, but because they don't enjoy being preachy. Maybe the more they know, the more they realize no one knows it all. They'll seldom say something has to be done a certain way, though there are definite taboos. More often, they spend their time listening, not lecturing. They're always on the prowl for some bit of expertise that can be added to their repertoire. Those knowledgeable in Corvette show-car preparation do what they do purely because they enjoy it. It's self-satisfaction. They don't mind if someone else cares or understands. They're almost always low-key types who enjoy talking about their craft only to people who honestly enjoy hearing what they have to say.

When the information does start to flow, stand back. They've forgotten more than most of us ever knew about detailing a Corvette. They have tricks and techniques they have developed or picked up over the years that they just do instinctively. But as they unload their warehouse of information, a familiar disclaimer keeps cropping up: "Now, this is the way I do it, but that doesn't mean there aren't better or faster ways. I just like this way because...."

The same sort of disclaimer applies to everything appearing in *Secrets*

Things that come apart easily and logically don't always go back together a week (or two years) later with the same ease and logic.

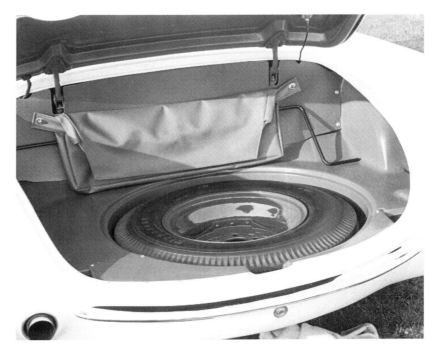

What was it before?

of Corvette Detailing. The consultants like and use the products mentioned, and these products achieve the desired results. But that's as far as any endorsement goes. There's nothing scientific here. No lab tests. No six month trials. Dave Burroughs swears by Dawn detergent for certain tasks, but he hasn't run side-by-side comparisons of every competitor's products. There might be products that work better than those we mention. All manufacturers mentioned in this text are receiving free plugs; endorsement money was neither offered nor accepted. In fact, the manufacturers would probably cringe and disclaim responsibility for some of the unorthodox ways our enthusiasts use their products anyway.

Documentation and order of battle

No matter how much or how little you intend to do to your Corvette, photographing what you're starting with is an excellent first step. There's bound to be some disassembly somewhere along the way, and having photos of the correctly assembled pieces can be a valuable reference. It's easy to take too much for granted during disassembly. Things that come apart easily and logically don't always go back together a week (or two years) later with the same ease and logic. Carburetor and fuel injection linkage are good examples, and there are lots of others. Which screw held this little gizmo in place? Which clamp was at the upper end of the hose and which at the lower? Which way were they turned? This bracket will fit two different ways, so which way is correct? Was this clip painted, plated, or raw?

Creating a documented record of what you started with is another reason for photographs. Pretend you're detailing for resale regardless of your intentions so you can put yourself in the place of a prospective buyer. Anyone looking at cosmetic perfection instinctively asks, "What was it before? Was a wreck skillfully pieced together?" Wrecked Corvettes deserve to be glued back together, but if you started with an unmolested Corvette and just improved it, doesn't it make sense to document that?

Yet another reason for documentation is that it might keep you from being sued, or worse, serving a jail term. Don't laugh. Back in the late

1980s, state and federal agents actually arrested enthusiasts who were either making or using reproduction materials to restore Corvettes. The charges revolved around either counterfeiting or fraud, and in most cases were terribly overblown. Parts counterfeiting, the practice of putting junk look-alikes in official-looking packaging, is a serious problem for auto companies. But in the Corvette world, discontinued components were being reproduced for restoration purposes. The whole mess was resolved when auto manufacturers, including General Motors, stepped in. They set up agencies to license legitimate individuals and companies to manufacture reproduction materials. The auto companies realized that it was clearly in their interests to encourage enthusiasm for their products.

Beyond action by state and federal authorities, you might hear now and then about one person suing another over a Corvette sale. Usually, these are big-money deals where the buyer claims to be a victim of fraud. For your own protection, remember the definition of fraud. It is the *intentional perversion of truth in order to induce another to part with something of value.* In a buy-sell transaction involving an automobile, it's not unusual for a seller to shade things positively. Shading is one thing. But if you switch trim tags on your Corvette to hide a color change, or restamp an incorrect engine and then misrepresent the Corvette to a buyer, you've committed fraud. I'm not saying you can't change your Corvette's color, or even change trim tags or engine stampings if you wish. You can. But you cannot misrepresent what you've done to a buyer. That is the *intentional* perversion of truth. I know people have gotten away with it for years. Dealers routinely spun speedometers back as part of their detailing operation for years, too. Some who couldn't break the habit spent time stamping out license plates in federal pens.

Protect yourself. Document your Corvette with photos before you do anything else. When you sell, you've got photographic proof showing what's been done. That, combined with a completely honest approach when selling, gives you significant legal protection. Don't worry that your Corvette is not perfect. A bullet hole through the fender, a blown piston…these things are all part of an individual Corvette's history and personality. Fix them if you wish, but don't try to obliterate them from your Corvette's history. This business of recreating bogus "original" thirty-year-old, 5,000-mile Corvettes could be the death of the hobby yet. Don't be part of it.

What sort of camera should you use? Articles on classic car care and restoration often recommend buying one of the inexpensive instant cameras. These inexpensive models are limited in their capabilities. In order to get in close to something like carburetor linkage, you'll need to upgrade to a higher-quality instant camera to provide satisfactory detail. Polaroid has refined instant photo technology to the point where some of its products do a fine job.

Over the years, I've purchased a couple of instant cameras because the ability to see what you've shot almost immediately is an attractive inducement. But I wind up not using them. Maybe it's just habit, but I keep going back to 35mm. For ultraconvenience, say walking around a Corvette show, I carry a small point-and-shoot 35mm that fits in my shirt pocket. I'm currently using an Olympus Stylus. It is fully automatic with a 35–70mm zoom lens and a little flash unit that pops up and fires when necessary. It replaced an equally small Yashika with a Zeiss lens that actually yielded a sharper image but didn't have a zoom. Lots of these small cameras are on the market, and most do a remarkably good job, considering their size and convenience. They will do just fine for documenting your

Protect yourself. Document your Corvette with photos before you do anything else.

Right and below: It's easy to think of older models as being the most important to carefully document before beginning detailing or restoration, but shouldn't the same be true of newer Corvettes, too? This 1990 ZR-1 is a complex piece of machinery. Its engine was meticulously built by Mercury Marine in Stillwater, Oklahoma, and its underhood assembly is pure artistry to Corvette enthusiasts. Photo documentation will help preserve the correct original appearance long into the future.

Corvette. However, call me old-fashioned, but my personal preference for that task is my old Nikon FM 35mm, a single-lens reflex, manual camera with a good built-in light meter and an excellent depth-of-field preview. The depth-of-field preview permits me to see exactly what will be in focus, and the single-lens reflex design shows me exactly what will be in the shot. The farther away you are, the less these things matter. But for tight closeups, dig out your old 35mm, or borrow your neighbor's.

When I shoot photos for a publication such as this one, I use either black and white negative film or color slide film. I love the subtle tones of black and white photography (no colorized *Casablanca* for me), and in the earlier edition of this book I suggested that readers consider black and white for documenting their Corvettes. I've changed my mind about that. Color print film is the best bet for documenting. One-hour processing is common practically everywhere, so it's hard to beat the convenience. Slide film does give the truest color and sharpest detail, but who wants to look through a viewer or drag out a projector? What is most helpul here is some sort of a quick reference album.

You might wish to use your personal computer to put together a presentation along with photos, which opens the possibility of yet another type of camera altogether, the digital. A digital camera does not use film at all, but instead records a digital image on internal memory. The image can then be transferred into a document created by any number of different software programs. Of course, you can accomplish the same thing with a flatbed scanner. That is, you can scan prints into digital images and place them into your computer-generated documents. This is another point in favor of using print film, as flatbed scanner technology is simple and good-quality flatbed scanners are very inexpensive. Good scans from negative or positive film require either an attachment for flatbed scanning or a stand-alone film scanner, either solution adding expense. If this is something you won't be doing often, rather than buy a scanner, you can use a service bureau or do it yourself at a computer rental facility.

Clearly, you shouldn't limit your documentation to photography. Even if you don't do a presentation using a PC, at least include written notes and sketches. Observations can be spoken into a tape recorder. If you have a little Steven Spielberg in you, consider videotape. The point is, documentation can't be overdone. Just last week, I sold a car to a gentleman who based his decision in no small part on the stack of paper and photos that went with the car and documented its history.

It is also good to obtain as much published data as possible. No other marques have as much printed material available as do Corvettes. Original or reprinted owner's manuals are available for all models. Factory assembly manuals, prepared by Chevrolet engineers to show assembly plant personnel how to put Corvettes together, are available in reprinted form for nearly all models built through 1982. These show minute details such as the correct sequence of washers between specific bolts and nuts. Service manuals are available for all Corvettes from the mid-1960s to the present. There are many excellent Corvette books written by enthusiasts. Add previously published materials to your own photos, notes, and the like, and you're off to an excellent documentation start. Don't be intimidated by any of this. Do what you feel comfortable with and enjoy, and it will greatly add to the appreciation and enjoyment of your Corvette. Selling it later at a higher price is icing on the cake.

When you finish your documentation to your satisfaction, you may be ready to start detailing. Then again, maybe not. The determining factor is the mechanical condition of your Corvette. There's little point in

Documention cannot be overdone.

Right: More Corvette artistry, circa 1955.

detailing an engine compartment if old gaskets are allowing oil and fuel to dribble and seep, or if the cylinder heads will be removed soon for a valve job. It is easier to do mechanical work on a detailed Corvette, but the work does spoil some detailing. Plan to get the mechanical fixes you're aware of out of the way before getting serious about cosmetics.

Once repairs are completed, I prefer to start with engine and chassis detailing. Even with protective covers in place, you'll scuff the exterior a little while working in the engine compartment. I do the interior next and save the exterior for last. For me, the exterior is the most fun. It certainly has the most impact. But there's really nothing sacred about the order.

Interior and exterior detailing will be presented in separate chapters, but these can be combined. For example, you could start by thoroughly cleaning the exterior, moving to the interior, then finishing with exterior detailing. If you have a crew working with you in a concours setting, interior and exterior can be done simultaneously.

This book's format is simple enough. There are separate chapters for engine and chassis detailing, interior detailing, exterior detailing, and long-term care. Compared with the previous edition, the most revisions and additions are found in the exterior and long-term care chapters. In the exterior section, new products and techniques (new to this book anyway) are included. The long-term care chapter has a lot more information about synthetic lubricants and other products and practices that can keep your Corvette alive and well indefinitely.

Some of these products can be dangerous. Be careful.

Speaking of products and practices, pay close attention to the warnings printed on the packages of things you use. Some of these products can be dangerous. Some can cause explosions in certain combinations. Some give off potent vapors you can inhale even while working outside. Some can demolish your skin. Be careful.

Repeating something said earlier, the products mentioned in this book haven't been chosen based on scientific analysis, and they are certainly not all-inclusive. They are simply those that I, or those who contributed to this book, have found to work well. The appendix provides the addresses, phone numbers, and web sites for manufacturers and suppliers of products mentioned in this text, except for products commonly available in auto stores, hardware stores, and supermarkets.

Now, let's get started.

Chapter 2

Engine & chassis detailing

The difference in detailing approach for Corvettes compared with other cars is most evident in the areas of engine and chassis. Here's where the wrong things, done with the best intentions, can seriously devalue a Corvette.

Observations

In the first edition of this book, I related some personal observations about a Pontiac GTO show I'd stumbled onto at a local mall. I was crazy about the GTO when it first came out and years later owned a 1965, so I was eager to see what these enthusiasts were doing compared with the Corvette crowd.

What I saw were cars beautifully prepared with great care. But what a difference in preparation between those Pontiacs and what was considered correct in the Corvette hobby. Under the hood, everything was either repainted or chromed, including components that certainly didn't have paint or chrome surfaces originally. Everything black was the same shade of black. Lots of small parts, things like brake line clips, brake fluid reservoir lids, and hose clamps, were spray-painted silver, even though parts like these usually came from the factory with cadmium or zinc plating or no finish at all.

There was a time, in the 1960s and early 1970s, when you would have seen the same thing at Corvette shows, especially small, local events. But not now. In saying this, I don't mean to demean those wonderful GTOs or to single out any marques as being restored or detailed badly. With all due respect, the multizillion dollar cars at the Pebble Beach Concours d´Elegance are grossly overrestored and overdetailed. This really is Corvette versus the world.

There is also the matter of personal taste. Some people avoid the Corvette hobby because they just don't agree with the approach. At that

This really is Corvette versus the world.

Above: It would be tempting to replace this 1966 427's painted valve covers with chromed covers. Chevrolet did just that for Corvette show cars of the era. Chevrolet executives changed to chrome for their personal cars. But factory build called for painted covers and that's the way they should stay. The goal is to figure out what the factory did and then to try to replicate or maintain that as closely as possible.

GTO show, casual observers were most in awe of the most egregious examples of overdetailing. Since serious attention to attractive engine compartment packaging by manufacturers is relatively new, it is understandable that some enthusiasts want to improve the factory look, because the factory look wasn't all that great. They want to do it the way they think the factory *should* have done it.

Detailing and restoration books don't help either. I've yet to read a non-Corvette restoration book that accurately portrays restoration as returning something to an original state. One detailing book I looked at actually recommends strip-cleaning the engine compartment, repainting the engine block in the original color, and then spray-bombing the rest in gloss black or silver, as you wish.

Over the years since that GTO show experience, the non-Corvette shows I've attended have pretty much confirmed the same observations. Certainly some-high quality restorations of high-line marques like Porsche, Ferrari, and Mercedes do pay close attention to refurbishing components in their original finishes, but even these tend to seek a level of perfection unlikely to have been produced by factory craftsmen on their best days.

Corvette enthusiasts have been moving away from overrestoration and overdetailing of chassis and engine components for some time. The goal now is a factory look. Exactly what duplicates correct factory appearance will always be subject to some debate, but this is just refining the goal. As you detail your Corvette's chassis and engine, be conservative.

Start with a thorough cleaning of the engine compartment. You may need to go no further.

Gentle cleaning

Don't make the mistake of assuming you'll need a warehouse of equipment before starting a detailing project. Steam cleaners, sandblasters, glass-beading cabinets, and drums of degreasing acid can all be useful, but they may be too destructive. They'll remove what you want to remove and then some. Granted, there are times when there is no choice. You'll be forced to use whatever technique or equipment is required to get a badly deteriorated surface back to where it can be refurbished, refinished, or replated. But many times, a gentle cleaning technique will bring an awful-looking engine compartment back to life, because some of the worst-looking engine compartments are the ones that look like everything was dunked in oily goo. The oily goo may have been the perfect preservative for the paint, labels, decals and codes beneath. It's the dry engine, the one

That oily goo may have been the perfect preservative.

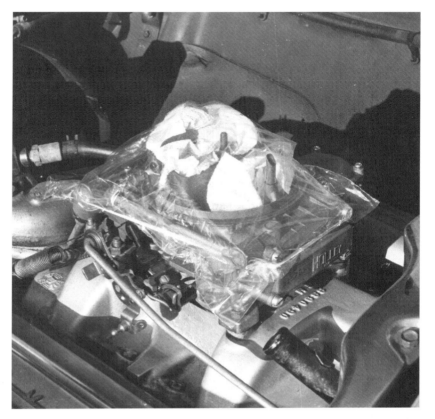

Page 24 top: The vinyl gloves you'll want for Corvette detailing are called vinyl examination gloves. These have a nicer fit and feel than similar products sold in hardware store paint departments. The three brands shown here, each slightly different but all excellent, were purchased at an auto body repair supply outlet, at a drug store, and from Griot's Garage mail order company. Be aware that these gloves have a light coating of a talc-like powder to make them slip on and off more easily, so it's a good idea to put the gloves on and then wash the power off if powder transfer could be a problem—holding a small part while painting, for example.

Page 24 center: Sal Ricotta uses glass cleaner to put a finishing touch on his 1969's air cleaner. Sal wears vinyl gloves to avoid fingerprinting the plated surface.

Above right: Prevent water from entering the carburetor by stuffing clean rags into the throats and covering with clear plastic sealed with rubber bands.

Above: Dawn dishwashing detergent is an excellent choice for gentle engine and chassis cleaning. Rustoleum's Rust Reformer is one of many such products that chemically converts rust to a protective coating without sanding. It will stop a small rusty nick on a frame member from spreading.

that looks like it was left in a field to rust, that leaves no choice but to use the harsh and abrasive stripping routine.

As a first step, start your cleaning with comfortably warm water, a variety of soft bristle brushes, some old washcloths, and a good grease-dissolving dishwashing detergent. This book series has always recommended Dawn, and I've yet to find anything better. Dawn's manufacturer, Proctor & Gamble, has introduced new varieties of the product over the years, such as a yellow lemon-scented variant. Suit yourself, but I still prefer the original blue formulation.

Squirt the detergent on full strength and go to work with your washcloths and soft brushes. The detergent will eat the grease and oil like magic, but the surface underneath will be unharmed if you don't scrub too aggressively.

Several passes may be required. Use your washcloth and fingers (latex or rubber gloves if you wish) gently on any labels, decals, or stenciled codes you uncover. If you brush or scrape too hard, these can be lost forever. Obviously, you must be especially cautious with paper labels, but be aware that the ink can be wiped off the foil type, too. Keep a garden hose handy for rinsing.

Steve Dangremond recently did a complete Corvette chassis cleaning by hand and related to me that thirty years of accumulated crud was taking too long with the method just described. Steve's first choice for this sort of project has always been Simple Green, but even that was too slow. He saw a product by Castrol called Super Clean at a local car parts store, so he tried that. He sprayed it on frame members full strength and let it soak in. Then he removed the softened buildup with a plastic putty knife. He

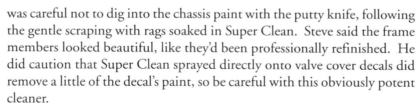

Left: Start gentle cleaning by hand with dishwashing detergent and sponges. Rinse carefully with a low-pressure hose.

Above and page 27: Products like Castrol's Super Clean and Spartan Chemical's BH-38 bridge the gap between gentle cleaning with a mild dishwashing solution and strong solvent cleaning with products like lacquer thinner. Super Clean and BH-38 are very potent cleaners when used undiluted, but both can be cut with up to ten parts water. Janitorial supply stores sell high quality, plastic squirt bottles like that shown above right. Use these to keep several different dilutions of Super Clean or BH-38 on hand.

was careful not to dig into the chassis paint with the putty knife, following the gentle scraping with rags soaked in Super Clean. Steve said the frame members looked beautiful, like they'd been professionally refinished. He did caution that Super Clean sprayed directly onto valve cover decals did remove a little of the decal's paint, so be careful with this obviously potent cleaner.

To be fair to Castrol, Super Clean's container has the usual disclaimers, plus a chart for different dilutions depending on the task. Engines, tires, and underbodies are the only automotive uses that call for full strength.

All engine compartment and chassis components can be cleaned with steps like those just described. It sounds like it will take forever, but it won't. Just a couple of hours will make a big difference in an engine compartment. You can, of course, spend a lot longer. That chassis project of Steve's, described above, took place while the engine was out of the car, and Steve did the engine compartment and chassis with the body on. He spent about twenty hours just cleaning with Super Clean and used eight 24-ounce pump-spray containers. The car was a somewhat neglected but very original and untouched midyear Corvette. It deserved the effort.

Throughout this text, I'll describe cleaning techniques and cleaning products recommended by Dave Burroughs. Most appeared in this book's

earlier edition and are still valid. Dave owns Corvettes and never stops detailing them, but his restoration efforts are currently directed toward one of his two Stearman airplanes. Dave tells me that his exposure to airplane restorers has introduced him to new products. For example, his preference for almost all cleaning tasks is now BH-38, an industrial strength cleaner/degreaser made by Spartan Chemical Company. Airplane people call this product "pink soap," and Dave says it is incredibly versatile. Used undiluted, it is a very powerful cleaner and degreaser. Depending on the task, it can be diluted with up to ten parts of water. Dave keeps several pre-mixed dilutions handy in spray bottles. You're not likely to find BH-38 in auto stores or at your local airport. This product is found almost exclusively at janitorial supply stores.

It's still a good idea to try detergent before BH-38, Super Clean, steam cleaning, or brutal solvents like lacquer thinner. The preservation of what's underneath the crud, already mentioned, is one concern; preservation of your hands is another. Strong solvents like lacquer thinner are effective precisely because they dissolve things, skin and latex gloves included (I have neoprene gloves that can stand up to strong solvents, but they're thick and clumsy to use). The fumes can be nasty. Rags soaked in some solvents should be stored in a metal container or tossed outside, because they can spontaneously ignite.

Make no mistake—these solvents are useful. Right now, a half-dozen different solvents (3-M's General Purpose Adhesive Cleaner, lacquer thinner, acetone, trichloroethane, PPG's Acryli-Clean DX300 wax and grease remover, and denatured alcohol) in quart cans are lined up in my garage for special cleaning tasks. The point is simply that when something milder will work, use it. Another advantage of the detergent method is that it can be done in your driveway at a leisurely pace. If ignition parts get wet and your Corvette won't start, you can just walk away or roll it into the garage and worry about it later.

Detergent or BH-38 or Super Clean won't always work. If your Corvette's engine compartment and chassis have already been "detailed" and the factory labels, decals, and markings are long gone or wrong, you may have to start over with heavy-duty cleaning. Ironically, the engine compartments of Corvettes completely neglected by previous owners are often the ones that can be salvaged by gentle cleaning and light detailing. The most well-intentioned Corvette owners, thinking they were taking the best possible care of their Corvettes by frequently giving the engine compartments the high-pressure degreasing treatment, may instead have removed some of the Corvette's precious originality.

Where your Corvette has spent its life also greatly affects the condition of its chassis and engine compartment. The chassis of a Corvette that has been winter-driven in areas where roads are salted usually has surface rust that gentle cleaning won't touch. But, thanks to the warm, sometimes oily environment under the hood, the engine compartment may respond to simple cleaning even in a Corvette with chassis rust.

Heavy-duty cleaning

If circumstances require a more powerful cleaning, you have the choice of commercial cleaning or the do-it-yourself variety. They accomplish the

Where your Corvette has spent its life greatly affects the condition of its chassis and engine compartment.

same thing, but commercial cleaners use more powerful equipment, they're more destructive, and they're quicker. Unless you rent the equipment, commercial cleaning means you'll let someone else handle the task. Steam cleaning is the most common type of commercial engine compartment cleaning.

For the do-it-yourself, heavy-duty method without steam cleaning, buy a couple of engine-degreasing spray bombs (Gunk is well known and works fine) and drive over to the self-serve, spray-wand car wash. While you're waiting in line, spray the hot engine compartment with the degreaser and let it soak. Then blast away with the high-pressure wand. If there's a soap or engine wash cycle, use it. A couple of applications may be needed, and you may have to help it along by brushing during the soak cycles.

There are various precautions to consider, depending on how aggressive this cleaning is to be. The engine should be prevented from ingesting water through the carb or injectors, and the ignition system and all electronic parts should be kept as dry as possible. It would take a good dose of water into the combustion chamber to cause internal damage, but it's conceivable. A wet ignition isn't fatal, but it could prevent starting. Don't spray Gunk or any degreaser on an engine while it's running because fan blade turbulence could blow the degreaser back into your eyes (eye protection is good advice no matter what technique is used).

Speaking of a running engine, I should point out that my personal quickie technique for non-Corvette engine compartments at the do-it-yourself wash places used to be to leave the engine running and to avoid directing the water at the air cleaner opening or distributor. If the engine started to stumble, I backed off until it cleared up. I used this technique without hand brushing or a degreasing presoak. I no longer recommend

The ignition system and all electronic components should be kept as dry as possible.

Page 28 left: An old fuel stain on this 1967 Corvette's intake manifold was sprayed with disc brake cleaner.

Page 28 right: Gunk engine degreaser is available in a standard formulation and a foaming version. Use it only as a presoak for stubborn oil or grease. Aerosol brake cleaners are effective for many cleaning jobs and don't leave a residue. For the intake manifold, it was simply sprayed and mopped up with paper towels.

Page 29: The intake manifold after cleaning with disc brake cleaner and paper towels.

this approach. One engine quit to the extent that I had to get a AAA tow home. And my Chevy pickup developed strange intermittent symptoms that turned out to be corrosion in the distributor cap. It never stumbled when I washed the engine compartment, but I think it sucked a little moisture into the distributor each time. These days I don't let engines run while cleaning.

For this more conventional technique of steam cleaning or high-pressure wash of an engine while it's not running, it's a good idea to remove the air cleaner(s) and block the carburetor or fuel injection air intake with clean rags sealed with sheet plastic. Products like Saran Wrap flex nicely, but I think they're too thin. I prefer freezer bags. Seal off the distributor, but take the cap off later and make sure it is completely dry. Trust me, a little moisture goes a long way in there. Handy things to have along include dry, lint-free rags, twine, and rubber bands.

Whether the engine is running or not, don't get too close with the spray wand. Even with a non-Corvette I care less about, I can't bring myself to strip-clean an engine compartment. Pressures vary, but by keeping yourself and the wand 2 or 3 feet away, grease, battery crud, salt, and loose debris can be cleared away with no damage to paint, labels, or markings.

A couple of points to remember with engine degreasers: First, they smell. It's not terrible, but it is distinctive. It will linger a while, and some people dislike it enough to avoid these products. Second, degreasers are pretty potent and can stain your Corvette's finish. The formulations of most over-the-counter degreasers aren't strong enough to permanently stain exterior paint, but the safety margin can be increased by keeping the exterior of the car wet and flushed before, during, and after the engine compartment cleaning. What you must avoid is a glob of pure degreaser soaking into a dry exterior surface. Adequately thinned with water, the degreaser won't cause spotting.

To avoid using degreasers completely, you can use kerosene to clean what detergent misses. Just remember that kerosene is itself a solvent and it will attack the frame paint of older Corvettes and any other coating that is oil-based. With degreasers or kerosene, flush the engine compartment well with water. Then dry with old, well-used towels.

Mechanical fixes

Now that the engine compartment is clean, this is the time to make another mechanical component check and to make repairs before detailing starts. Check all rubber hoses. Some hoses deteriorate from the inside out, so an external visual check won't be conclusive. Still, looking at the ends will give a pretty good idea of a hose's condition. If a hose has to be replaced, don't remove the clamp and start yanking. The correct procedure is to carefully split the end of the hose with a sharp knife or single-edge razor blade. Then peel the hose off. Lubricate the new hose with a little soap so it will slip on easily.

While on the subject of hoses, here are a few pointers. If you suspect your Corvette's hoses are originals, save them even if they're bad. New hoses for virtually all Corvette models are available, but the markings on replacements will be different if a Corvette is more than a few years old. The markings are applied by the manufacturer and can be removed with lacquer thinner. No markings are better than incorrect markings. Even if you're not concerned with ultra-accuracy now, saving your original hoses will permit you to either duplicate the markings yourself later or be sure an NOS (new-old-stock) or reproduction hose correctly matches your original. Also, as John Amgwert points out, saving old hoses for comparison is important to ensure that the new hoses are the correct length. Often, they're not.

If you weren't sure how far you wanted to go at the start, now's a good time to stand back and admire your work. After the thorough, gentle cleaning, many Corvette engine compartments require little more. At a minimum, the hoses and wiring harnesses should get a silicone treatment, and you'll probably want to spruce up the exhaust manifolds.

More disassembly

It may be easier and more time-effective to disassemble some components for individual detailing. For example, the carburetor could be removed, thoroughly cleaned and rebuilt, and then put back in place. Chromed fuel lines can be removed and either cleaned or replated. If any painting is to be done, the more components removed the better. When aiming for concours, some disassembly is a certainty. The ultimate Corvette engine compartment detailing procedure is engine removal. For serious detailing approaching restoration, engine removal is faster than trying to work with the engine in place, especially for someone who's been through it before. It permits the engine to be repainted with the same spray patterns used at the engine assembly plant, and it's much easier to get at the engine compartment itself. But it does require some space, an engine hoist, and

Above: Lacquer thinner is an item that no car enthusiast should be without. For some tasks, nothing will work better. But this is a very destructive solvent. It will attack the factory-applied paint of every Corvette model from 1953 to present. The fumes are toxic in enclosed spaces. Latex gloves will stand up to lacquer thinner only briefly. The neoprene gloves shown are impervious to lacquer thinner, but these gloves are thick and clumsy to use.

Page 31: In the early days of NCRS judging, if it couldn't be seen, it wasn't judged. Now, owners are asked to remove some components so that judges can see the part—in the case of this air cleaner—and the numbers and codes otherwise hidden.

an engine stand, all of which can be rented. Let's briefly look at what's involved in an engine pull procedure, and then return to specific detailing steps that are applicable with or without engine pulls.

Pulling an engine the first time is intimidating. The best advice is to have a shop manual handy, take your time, and have someone close by who's been through it before. The first time I pulled a Corvette engine, I did it mostly alone in a dirt-floor garage, but a knowledgeable, Corvette-owning neighbor assisted at the critical moments and guided me through. A Chevrolet shop manual for mid-year Corvettes will outline a step-by-step procedure something like this:

1. Drain cooling system and crankcase.
2. Scribe line around hood hinges and remove hood.
3. Remove air cleaner and cover carburetor with cloth.
4. Remove distributor shielding.

The first time is intimidating.

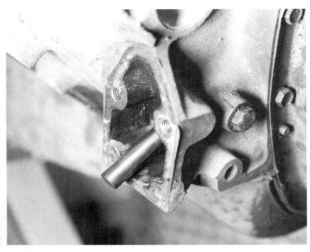

Top left: Temporarily replacing the bolt shown with one long enough to contact the fuel pump push rod will keep the rod in position for easy reinstallation of the pump.
Top: The fuel pump push rod will fall like this if it isn't temporarily held in place by a larger bolt. This makes later reinstallation of the fuel pump more difficult.
Left: Here is the temporary installation of the longer bolt to hold the fuel pump push rod in place before fuel pump removal.

5. Remove shroud and radiator as outlined.
6. Disconnect:
    a. Battery cables at battery.
    b. Wires at starter solenoid.
    c. Delcotron wiring.
    d. Engine-to-body ground straps.
    e. Oil pressure sensor at engine.
    f. Temperature sensor lead at sending switch.
    g. Coil primary lead at coil.
    h. Tachometer cable at distributor.
    i. Gas tank line at fuel pump.
    j. Accelerator rod at pedal bellcrank and TV rod (lower) at TV bellcrank.
    k. Heater hose at engine connections, and remove from clip at generator bracket.
    l. Power brakes hose at carburetor "t."
7. Remove fan and fan pulley assemblies.

Top: The Bowman brand is one of many engine enamels available for Chevrolet blocks. Flat black lacquer is less flat than enamel and doesn't mar like enamel. It works well for certain engine and chassis detailing tasks.

Top right: Some freeze plugs, like this one normally hidden under a motor mount, are difficult to replace when an engine is installed. When an engine is out of a Corvette, be sure to check all freeze plugs carefully. Replace any that are suspect or better yet, replace them all.

The appropriate shop manual always spells out the correct procedure.

8. Power steering only:
   a. Remove power steering pump mount bolts and swing pump into radiator opening.
   b. Or, disconnect pump lines and plug open ends.
9. Remove rocker arm covers.
10. Remove distributor cap, move it forward of distributor and cover distributor with a cloth.
11. Raise vehicle and place on jack stands.
12. Disconnect exhaust pipes at manifold flanges.
13. Remove oil filter.
14. Block clutch pedal in up position. Then remove clutch cross shaft (frame bracket end first, then slide off engine ball stud).
15. Remove starter assembly.
16. Remove flywheel cover plate (synchromesh) or converter underpan (Powerglide).
17. Remove engine front mount through bolts.
18. Position a floor jack under transmission. Then remove all but top two bellhousing-to-engine bolts.
19. Install engine lift tool; then remove two upper bellhousing bolts.
20. Powerglide only: Remove flywheel-to-converter bolts and install converter holding bracket to transmission.
21. Raise and move engine forward alternately as needed to remove engine from vehicle.
22. Install engine on engine stand and remove lift tool assembly.

As mentioned, this procedure list is for a midyear Corvette, as some clues (Powerglide, tach cable at distributor) indicate. The exact procedure varies for different models, but the appropriate shop manual always spells out the correct procedure.

Not to stray too far from detailing, but while on this subject, Don Williams wanted to pass along some classic small-block engine-pulling advice. Don prefers to remove the exhaust manifolds, plugs, fuel pump, and starter before pulling the engine. To keep the fuel pump's push rod shaft in place when the pump is removed, temporarily replace the bolt on the forward face of the block with a longer one that will contact the push

Left: The home closet can yield some useful items for Corvette detailing. Here, an old sock is being worn as a glove and is used for cleaning and polishing.

Page 35: Again raiding the closet, a pair of lady's underwear protects this Corvette's undercarriage from jackstand scratches. No further comment required.

rod. Do this after rotating the crank so the engine is set to fire the #1 cylinder. It you don't do this, it makes it more difficult to replace the fuel pump. Put the original bolt back in later and seal it with gasket cement. Also, Don reminds us that draining the radiator doesn't drain the block. To avoid a mess later, drain the block by removing the lowest freeze plug. Check the condition of all other freeze plugs while the engine is out. Prudence dictates just replacing them all.

Painting

If engine surfaces are to be repainted, use an original-type engine enamel. Spray bombs are available. The factory sprayed Corvette engines while suspended in an almost fully assembled state. Components like the intake and exhaust manifolds, valve covers, and oil pan were usually in place. If the intake was to be natural or painted silver, or if the valve covers were aluminum, these were masked, but not all that carefully. The majority of Corvette exhaust manifolds over the years have been raw cast iron (newer Corvettes have stainless steel) with no finish whatever other than engine enamel, most of which quickly burned off when the engine came up to operating temperature.

Corvette detailers nearly always do a nicer job than the factory did. Some range of quality is acceptable because the factory's quality varied. You can do a very neat job and still have a legitimate factory look if you

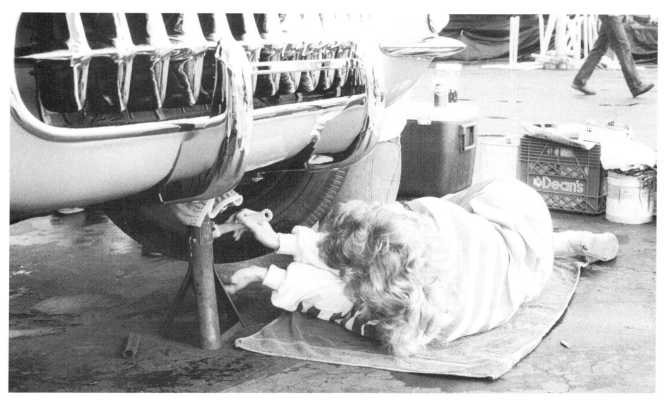

You can learn a lot by scrutinizing each part carefully before removing its finish.

pay attention to details, especially gaskets. One giveaway that a Corvette has had engine components detailed individually while disassembled in a nonfactory procedure is the gasket edges. For example, factory-original engine gaskets would have paint left on their edges. If you want the Bloomington Gold look, you'll need to have some paint on the gasket edges, even if you detail the components individually while disassembled.

Don't use flat black enamel of the hardware store variety to respray the inner fender wells or black chassis components. The factory didn't use it. It might look nice right after it's sprayed, but it will mar every time it's touched. Further, a monotone look with everything the same shade of black—the frame, fender wells, little clips, and brackets—looks phony. It is just not the way Corvettes looked when built. Why? For one thing, because many Corvette components were supplied by independent vendors who used different kinds of paints and finishes. Speaking of the pre-1984 models, frames came into the Corvette assembly plant already painted with petroleum-based paint that will thin with kerosene or gasoline. Chevrolet workers sprayed the fender wells with a flattish chassis black, but it wasn't the same material as the frame paint. Clips and brackets had all sorts of finishes—some gloss, some flat, some sprayed, some dipped, and some plated.

Here's where your own research comes in. If your Corvette is fairly original, you can learn a lot by scrutinizing each part carefully before removing its finish. If there isn't enough left to tell, or if what's there is wrong, you can gather the information by visiting quality Corvette shows, viewing similar Corvettes, and keeping your eyes and ears open. Now you can appreciate why I so strongly recommend initially cleaning your Corvette without using destructive methods.

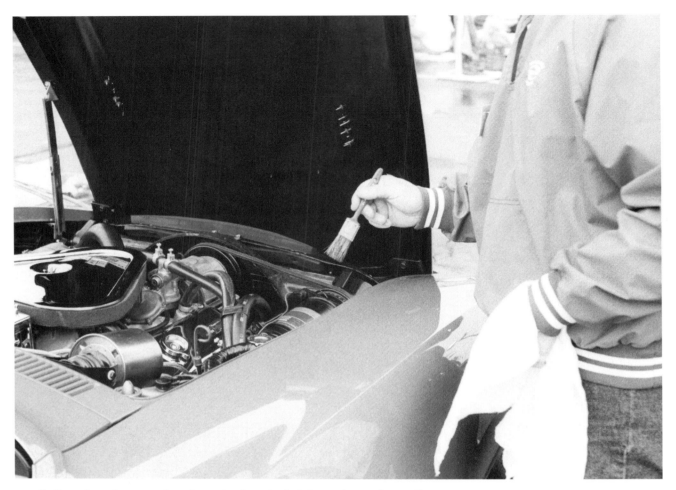

Before throwing your hands up in despair, let's be realistic about all this. In a complete factory-type restoration or detailing involving repainting, it isn't possible to duplicate factory finishes *exactly*. Even if you could locate the original manufacturer of every painted engine compartment and chassis component and find out the formula of the paints they used, some of these materials would be unavailable because of health hazard restrictions subsequently imposed. Moreover, different vendors may have supplied the same parts with different finishes during the same model year, or the same vendor may have changed paints during the same model year. Whew!

Do the best you can. Research your own car, research others like it, get a comfortable feel for what is acceptable, and then proceed. A Bloomington Gold or NCRS judge may not agree with what you've done, and maybe you'll have to redo something. The arguments about what the factory did and didn't do will never end, but that's all part of the fun. With this attitude, your best shot will put you far ahead of those detailing other marques.

Brightwork

The best way to handle engine component chrome and brightwork is to remove it and clean it by hand in a sink using dishwashing detergent and a fine grade of steel wool. Once cleaned, apply several coats of paste

It isn't possible to duplicate all factory finishes exactly.

Page 36: Every Corvette concours entrant's equipment bag includes a variety of brushes. Used dry, simple brushes will sweep dust into a little pile where it can be picked up with a ball of tape, or a lint-free towel dampened with glass cleaner.

Top and right: Concours enthusiasts go all out for concours display. These solid aluminum supports suspend this 1963 Corvette coupe safely for detail preparation. For actual concours, most shows do require that Corvettes be judged with wheels and tires in place.

wax. Engine compartments are harsh environments for plated surfaces, so these have to be attended to regularly to maintain their attractiveness. If plating has deteriorated too far, the choice is to replate or replace. There isn't much cost advantage to replating, but I prefer it because it keeps the original part in place. Some of the dinkiest little parts have codes that correctly date them to the car. Hundreds of components in every Corvette are date-coded in some way.

Above: It is easy to make engine compartment rubber look great. Here an upper radiator hose was cleaned with solvent and protected with silicone. This was a replacement hose with incorrect markings, so lacquer thinner was used to remove them. For an original hose, a much milder cleaning procedure should be used.

Wiring harnesses, hoses, and other rubber

Individual wiring and wiring harnesses will usually come clean with the detergent treatment. If not, try PPG's Acryli-Clean DX 330. Don't soak with Acryli-Clean, as the wire insulation coating or harness wrapping could be damaged. Rub it on lightly so that the stains are removed and the solvent quickly evaporates. Come back with a Dawn detergent bath

Above: PPG's Acryli-Clean (formerly Ditzler's) is a great cleaner, yet it won't damage painted surfaces. Carburetor cleaner is thought of as excellent for removing gum and varnish deposits inside carburetors, but it also works well for external fuel stains on intake manifolds. High temperature paints are formulated to withstand exhaust manifold temperatures. Several varieties are available, but "cast iron" comes closest to the original finish of cast iron manifolds.

once more. Then coat with full-strength silicone protectant. Don't drench it, but let a light surface coating remain for several hours before wiping with a soft cloth. You'll be amazed.

If rubber hoses don't require replacement, they can be made to look like new using the same technique just described for the wiring. Lacquer thinner is also great for hoses; however, if hoses are original and still have the markings, don't use lacquer thinner because it will dissolve the markings. A gentle detergent washing will usually be adequate. Acryli-Clean won't dissolve markings as quickly as lacquer thinner, but clean carefully. Either way, follow with an application of silicone or a commercial rubber preservative. The rubber lubricant that gas stations use for a new tire bead before mounting works well and also leaves a nice, protective finish. It's available at specialty stores in pint or quart cans.

Manifolds

Intake manifolds always need attention if carburetors or fuel injection connections have been leaking. For aluminum intakes, caution is advised in the cleaning stage. Glass beading or sandblasting will definitely clean the surface, but it may also change the surface texture. Instead, try soaking in paint stripper. Gas stains, grease, and paint overspray will be gobbled up, but the aluminum won't be affected. Use a nonmetallic-bristle brush to loosen the stubborn stains; then flush with water. For later maintenance of a gas stain, direct a squirt of disc brake cleaner at the stain with one of the readily available spray bombs, and sop up with a paper towel. A squirt of carburetor cleaner will also work.

Cast-iron exhaust manifolds are invariably the worst-looking components in a Corvette's engine bay. Virtually any paint will burn off exhaust manifolds due to the searing heat, so Chevrolet never made any pretense about trying to give these a permanent finish. Usually, exhaust manifolds got a dose of engine enamel along with the block. This enamel had a higher temperature tolerance than normal enamel, of course, but not nearly enough to last long on manifolds. Other than a crevice here and there, the paint soon burned off the manifolds and they took on a layer of surface rust.

The technique for exhaust manifolds used today by detailing shops and espoused in other books is to refinish with super-high-temperature manifold paint, which does last pretty well. The most natural I've seen is VHT's "hi-temp Nu-Cast manifold coating" #SP998, a 1,500°F paint that has an appearance close to cast iron. If painting is the route, an alternative is high-temperature clear, though it is too glossy for a natural look.

There is also a technique called Porcelainizing, a moderately expensive ceramic coating that will last. It leaves a much nicer looking surface than the original.

The problem with all the finishes mentioned is that either they don't look right or they don't last or both. If we apply the factory-original guideline here, the correct appearance is raw cast iron with traces of engine enamel. Dave Burroughs thinks a trace of rust is natural and okay for Bloomington judging.

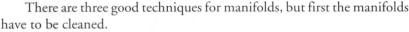

There are three good techniques for manifolds, but first the manifolds have to be cleaned.

Unbolting the manifolds for cleaning is a simple matter if you've removed your Corvette's engine. If not, you can still remove the manifolds. Having them off the engine will result in the best job, but you can also get acceptable results if you leave them on. Personally, I would not remove them solely for cleaning and refinishing.

Manifolds off the engine can be cleaned quickly to bare metal by sandblasting, glass beading, or an acid dip. You can also wire-brush them yourself if you don't have the other equipment and don't feel like taking them to someone else. A bench-mounted wire brush attachment on a grinder works great because the manifolds can be moved across the brush face. Or the manifold can be mounted in a vise and attacked with a handheld wire brush or with a brush attachment on an electric drill.

You'll need more time if you're cleaning the exhaust manifolds while they're on the engine in the car. You can use an electric drill with a wire brush for some areas, but be careful. It's best to clean with small brass-bristle brushes. Start with naval jelly to dissolve the rust and then follow with detergent. SOS pads are useful, too. Stuff rags under and around the manifolds to catch the residue and drippings if you need to protect the rest of the engine compartment. Take special care where the manifolds bolt to the block. Work slowly.

Regardless of the cleaning technique, it is important to get rid of all the residue. Little pieces of SOS pads, sand, or glass particles can remain

Above left: If exhaust manifolds are removed, they can be cleaned with a wire brush attachment on a bench grinder. Protective clothing, including safety glasses and gloves, should be worn.
Above: Naval jelly dissolves rust and is a good first step in cleaning exhaust manifolds. SOS has many roles in heavy-duty cleaning jobs, exhaust manifolds being one of them.

Above: After wire brushing and SOS and lacquer thinner cleaning—it is very important to remove every trace of SOS—this manifold was coated with silicone protectant. Several coats and "burn ins" give an excellent and natural finish. But it is not permanent and must be renewed often.

embedded in a manifold that, at first glance, appears perfectly clean.

Here are three different methods for achieving a natural-looking cast iron finish on clean exhaust manifolds:

1. The first technique is the automotive equivalent to grandma's seasoning of cast-iron skillets with cooking oil. Give the clean manifolds a clean rinse with the hottest water you can stand. Let the manifolds air-dry (it won't take long) and then drench with Armor All. Let soak for a day. Then install and burn in by letting the engine warm up. The Armor All will bead and dance on the manifold surface. Apply more to the hot manifolds and continue doing so until it starts to absorb. Let the engine cool, and wipe off the excess. You won't believe the results. The manifolds will look like virgin castings, but without discoloration or rust. There's just one catch. It won't last. The beads will appear to some extent whenever

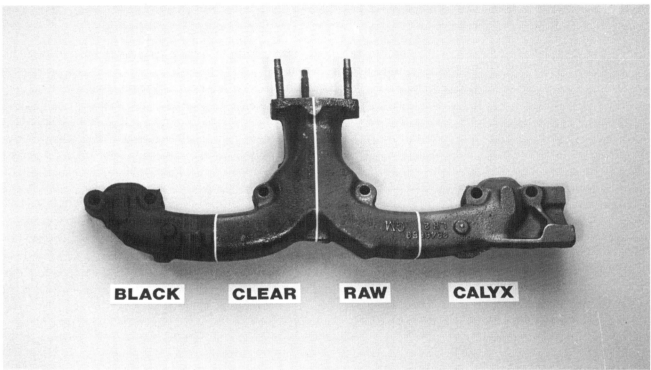

BLACK **CLEAR** **RAW** **CALYX**

the manifolds get hot, and the process has to be repeated. It is not practical for a street car, but it gives a natural cast-iron look that's nice for a show car or seldom-driven garage dweller.

2. The second technique is to apply Calyx Manifold Dressing to the clean manifolds. This is a paste with graphite and some mystery ingredients. You can apply it with your finger or a rag. (I do both, but wear latex gloves). It can be left as is or buffed with newspaper, flannel, or a shoebrush for a bit of gloss. It won't burn off, but since it is water soluble, it does have to be touched up now and then. The manufacturer says it lasts from 5,000 to 8,000 miles on a street-driven Corvette, indefinitely on a show car. The graphite in Calyx Dressing produces a slightly more gray appearance than the virgin part would have. But it is still very good, and is probably the most popular manifold product among enthusiasts who show Corvettes.

In fact, while Calyx Manifold Dressing is used on many cars besides Corvettes, it is interesting to note that Calyx Corporation president George Albright developed the product as a result of his own frustrations while showing his 1960 Corvette. It's one of many examples of ingenious

It won't burn off.

Page 42: A rusty exhaust manifold was cleaned and given three different finishes in addition to raw (no finish at all). Since this photo was staged, some paint manufacturers have introduced "cast iron" finish which is a better choice than either black or clear. In this demonstration, Calyx clearly provided the most natural-looking finish.

Right: *Calyx manifold dressing comes in this handy little plastic tub. It has the consistency of cold cream, contains graphite, and is applied with the fingers. It is easy to use and gives a natural finish, but it never completely dries and is water soluble, so periodic touchup is needed.*

Far right: *Hot Stuff is sold in a little tub similar to Calyx, but is a completely different product. It contains ceramic, and dries hard. Since it is brushed on, application technique is critical. It is very durable.*

products that have resulted from Corvette enthusiasts' relentless searches for something better.

3. Which brings us to the third method, another product developed by a Corvette enthusiast. Dick Barron, owner of Virginia Vettes, wanted a manifold dressing that cured hard and lasted. His product, Hot Stuff, is a blend of stainless steel and ceramic, and is said to withstand temperatures of 2,400°F. To put that into perspective, a searing hot manifold glowing cherry red is about 1,200°F.

Instructions for using Hot Stuff recommend applying a thin coat to a clean manifold with a small brush. Air-dry for two hours at room temperature. Then "set" by running the engine for ten minutes. If the manifold is off the engine, just cure it in an oven for an hour at 275°F.

The downside of Hot Stuff is that the result does not look quite as natural as either of the previous two techniques. (The best results are achieved by keeping the coating thin to minimize brush marks.) But the hard, durable aspect of this product is a big plus for street cars.

Dick Barron emphasizes the importance of using his product on a manifold that's been well cleaned. It is especially important to remove other products, like Calyx, before applying Hot Stuff.

Final touch

As a final touch, other detailing books advise spraying the entire engine compartment with clear lacquer. If you've shopped used-car dealers, you've seen it. I've passed on used cars with this treatment that I would have bought otherwise. Don't even consider it. Once engine and chassis components have been renewed to the correct appearance, nothing more is required.

Don't even consider it.

Chapter 3

Interior detailing

The materials and finishes found in a Corvette's interior vary from painted surfaces to metal, carpet, fabrics, vinyls or leathers, plastics, and even wood. Some of these require special care with special products. Others can be handled with everyday household products from the hardware store or supermarket.

Painted surfaces

Painted interior surfaces usually aren't subjected to extreme wear and often require no more than gentle cleaning with a scented household cleaner. If surfaces are damaged to the extent that refinishing is necessary, remove the pieces from the interior. Don't try to match interior paint at the hardware store. Corvette product suppliers have packaged the more popular colors in spray bombs. For less common colors, exact duplicates or acceptable matches can be mixed by a local auto paint jobber. Some auto paint jobbers can make spray bombs for you in any color, and others sell a little spraying kit with a can of compressed air and a jar for the paint. Either works reasonably well, so professional spraying equipment isn't necessary to get acceptable results on interior trim. Often, interior painting involves little pieces, and it's a hassle to fire up big equipment even if you have it.

Some concours entrants like to coat painted interior surfaces with a silicone protectant product, but my preference is to minimize the use of silicone in interiors. I sometimes use it for rubber, but little else. More on this later.

Vinyl

Vinyl interior components can be cleaned with any number of products. Non-abrasive household cleaners like Dow Bathroom Cleaner, Simple Green and Murphy Oil Soap work nicely, and countless vinyl

Minimize the use of silicones in interiors.

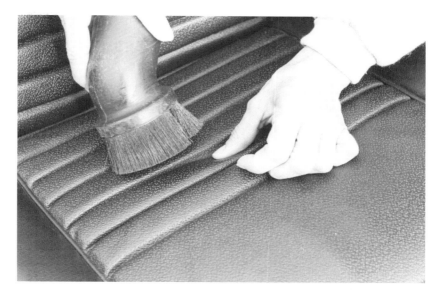

Above: Murphy Oil Soap, Dow Bathroom Cleaner with "scrubbing bubbles," and Simple Green are common household cleaners that clean interior Corvette surfaces very nicely.

Right: Use a powerful vacuum to clean Corvette seats, and help the vacuum by spreading pleats where dirt can hide. For thorough cleaning, some seat disassembly may be necessary.

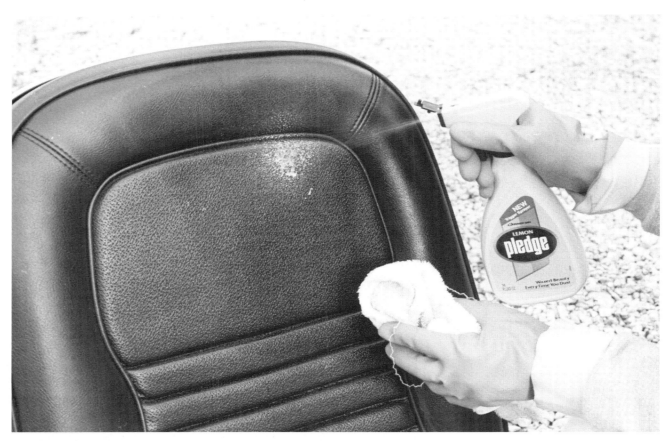

Top and bottom left: *Lemon-scent Pledge furniture polish is a favorite for Corvette interior vinyl. Don't forget the areas behind the trim pieces because this is where odors start and can hide.*

Above: *The classic treatment for leather is cleaning with saddle soap, followed by neatsfoot oil to replenish moisture.*

cleaners are sold in auto stores. Antibacterial household cleaners, Dow Bathroom Cleaner for example, contain some bleach or bleach substitute to kill bugs. Killing bugs is good, but the ingredients in these cleaners might spot some surfaces. As a general rule, when using any cleaner on a material for which that cleaner isn't specifically intended, test it first.

Once vinyl is clean, a pump-spray furniture polish such as Pledge leaves a nicely protected finish with some gloss, but without the wet look of a product like Armor All. Before using a silicone protectant on interior vinyl, be sure to read the section on silicone cautions later in this chapter. Leather cleaners and protectants can be used on vinyl, but vinyl products generally shouldn't be used on leather.

Leather

Compared with vinyl, leather demands considerable additional care. Leather is a natural material with oils that evaporate, causing it to crack and deteriorate if moisture is not maintained. On the other hand, too much moisture can cause other problems, including rotted stitching. Good leather cleaners and preservatives can be purchased from a hardware store, from any saddle or leather shop, and from any decent shoe repair shop. Because leather deterioration occurs over long spans of time and is obviously also dependent on the leather's inherent quality, it's difficult to evaluate the effectiveness of the different care products available. Of the speciality products I've tried, I like those offered by Lexol and IBIZ. Dave Burroughs likes Eagle 1 Leather Care and Conditioner.

What these specialized products are designed to do is simplify the time-proven technique of using saddle soap for cleaning followed by neatsfoot oil for preserving. The old saddle soap and neatsfoot oil route is more work than the one-step products, but you can still get excellent results if you're willing to invest the time.

Here's how. With a damp sponge, work up a little saddle soap foam and rub gently into the leather. Wipe the excess off and let it dry. Then thoroughly buff with a dry cloth. Saddle soap itself replenishes oils in the leather, and just using it may be sufficient. But if you want to really be sure the oils are replenished, or if the leather has stiffened by being subjected to wet-dry cycles, follow the saddle soap step (after the leather has dried) with a coating of neatsfoot oil. Let the oil soak in and then buff out the excess with a clean old towel. I do this periodically with a set of leather Recaro seats I've had for over twenty years, and the leather still looks beautiful. Unfortunately, the quality of leather specified for Corvette seats by Chevrolet over the years has been less than what one would expect in a car of this caliber. I recall the leather seats in my 1984 Corvette starting to show wear at 3,000 miles. This is good news only for companies that supply aftermarket seat recovering kits.

If the appearance of a Corvette's seat leather is poor but the leather itself is intact, it is possible to at least improve the appearance. A deteriorated leather surface without open splits or tears can be lightly sanded with 600-grit sandpaper to reveal a smooth, uncoated surface, followed by a spray or brush-on leather dye. The result will not be show quality by any stretch of the imagination, but for a driver it might suffice. Sometimes leather simply loses color due to abrasion, the best example

> **Too much moisture can cause other problems, including rotted stitching.**

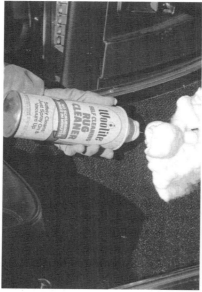

Left above: Woolite makes both a foaming carpet cleaner and a slightly different product for cleaning upholstery. Resolve carpet cleaner leaves a nice scent behind and also adds a stain repellent.
Left below: Foaming carpet cleaners are sprayed directly onto the carpet surface and then worked in. The safest way to do this is by hand because using a brush could tear the carpet fibers.

being the entry area of the driver's seat. If the color can be matched, try paste shoe polish. The excess polish must be completely buffed out or it will transfer to clothing. Follow the shoe polish with neatsfoot oil and buff again. This is a touch-up technique not suitable for large seating areas because of the color transfer problem. In my teenage years, I once changed the tan leather bench seats in a Studebaker coupe to black using nothing but shoe dye and polish. I was really proud of myself, because that seat looked fantastic. But for many months, whatever clothing I or my passengers wore picked up a little black polish. Not good.

Carpet and fabric

Excellent household products are available at hardware stores, supermarkets, and auto stores for cleaning Corvette carpeting. The best of the do-it-yourself products is spray foam that is applied directly to carpet, worked in, allowed to dry, and then vacuumed out. My favorite

The excess polish must be buffed out.

48

Right: Trichloroethane is a replacement for carbon tetrachloride and is useful for removing tar or small stains from carpet or fabric upholstery.
Far right and below: Rub foaming carpet cleaner into carpet until it almost disappears. Let it dry, then vacuum. Wipe cleaner overspray off trim pieces with a damp rag. Don't mask unless you're sure the surface being masked is stable.

Consider stealing a little yarn from under the seat.

for years was made by Woolite, and I also like their upholstery cleaner, another foaming product that is great for cleaning seat and door panel fabrics. My new favorite for carpet is Resolve. All foaming carpet cleaners probably clean equally well, but I like the pleasant odor Resolve leaves behind. Plus, it has a stain-repellent built in. I buy it at a local supermarket.

If your Corvette has closed-loop carpeting, don't use a brush to work the cleaner into the carpet because brushing will tear the loops slightly and give it the fuzzies. Use your hand, a sponge, or part of an old towel. Always vacuum first. Dave Burroughs pounds the carpet with one hand while vacuuming with the other to make dirt "jump" up to where the vacuum can get it.

Carpeting can always be brought back to life provided there aren't tears or worn spots. For a small, isolated wear spot like a heel rest, consider stealing a little yarn from under the seat and carefully patching. John Amgwert uses a fingernail clipper to trim carpet fuzzies and excess threads.

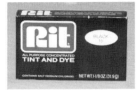

Left and left below: For removing the last traces of surface dirt and lint from carpet, make a small loop from duct tape, adhesive side out. Then roll the loop around the carpet by hand.
Above: Corvette aftermarket suppliers make vinyl paint for many Corvette interior colors. It is designed for vinyl, but can also be used for light carpet touchup. Household dyes like Rit can be used for black carpet touchup, but most other Corvette colors can't be matched very well.

For stains in fabric or carpeting, John recommends lighter fluid but cautions against rubbing the fluid directly on the stain. John's technique is to lay a clean rag on the stain, and then rub that rag with another soaked in lighter fluid. The stain will be drawn up into the first rag rather than just spread around the fabric. Years ago, carbon tetrachloride was a popular stain remover. My dad always kept it around for removing tar that found its way to car and home carpet when neighborhood streets were resurfaced. But carbon tet's fumes were toxic, and it is unavailable now for consumer

Lay a clean rag on the stain, then rub that first rag with another soaked in lighter fluid.

Secrets of Corvette Detailing

Above: It's one of the best-known household products, but sometimes overlooked for automotive use. Use Scotchgard for protecting Corvette carpeting and cloth upholstery after cleaning.

The tan paint came right off the console when the masking tape was removed.

use. A less dangerous substitute called Carbo Chlor (trichloroethane) is available in hardware stores.

In the late 1960s when I was driving a black-interior midyear Corvette daily, I used a spray dye called Fabspray to renew its carpeting. It was a great product, but I can no longer find it or any other spray product designed specifically for carpet that works as well. Corvette speciality companies sell spray vinyl dyes that work pretty well for carpeting. Dave Burroughs has had limited success mixing his own dye for black carpeting using household products like Rit, but other colors didn't work well. This is one reason I've always preferred a pure black interior to the charcoals and grays common nowadays. Dave now prefers to clean original carpeting the best he can and to then leave it alone.

Other restorers have dusted carpets with lacquer or other paints. In any case, remember that a carpet's color can be improved, but the color can't really be changed. When using a spray product on carpet, work it into the carpet fibers with a lintless rag or sponge before it dries. Otherwise, a hard crust will remain on top of the fibers. Even in the best of cases, the carpet won't be as soft after you've dosed it with paint or vinyl dye.

After carpeting or seat and door panel fabric is cleaned to your satisfaction, protection can be enhanced with a stain repellent like Scotchguard. At a cost of $10 or so, a complete Corvette interior can be protected. Don't do what I did with my very first new Corvette, though. I had my 1984 about a week when I decided to protect the carpeting from stains. So I masked off the console, sprayed the Scotchguard, and pulled the tan paint right off the console when I removed the tape. What a feeling. Just hold a piece of cardboard as an overspray shield.

For concours preparation, when every speck of lint must be removed from carpeting, Don Williams suggests making a loop from about a foot of 2-inch duct tape, sticky side up, and rolling the loop round the carpet with your hand. Works great for sweaters, too.

Rubber

Door and glass seals and other rubber can be made to look like new with little effort. Clean with detergent first. If that's not enough, PPG's Acryli-Clean DX 330 works wonders with rubber. Lacquer thinner also cleans rubber beautifully, but use it as a last resort. A stray dribble will eat anything in its way, and it could weaken old rubber. Whatever you use, dampen a rag and work small areas of the rubber (you can be less careful with detergent or Acryli-Clean). After cleaning, apply rubber lubricant or silicone protectant as a preservative. Don't squirt the protectant directly onto interior rubber. Apply it to a rag, then use the rag to apply the protectant. Here's one situation where buffing will remove gloss, so continue to buff with dry rags until the rubber has a natural sheen. Also, try diluting your silicone protectant with equal parts or more of water. I bought a gallon of Armor All at a car show ages ago, and then mixed diluted solutions in squirt bottles. I'm still using them. It's often not necessary to use silicone protectants full strength.

The steps just described also work great on windshield wipers, making them look and function almost like new. As a bonus, the added flexibility sometimes cures windshield wiper squawk-and-jitter across the glass.

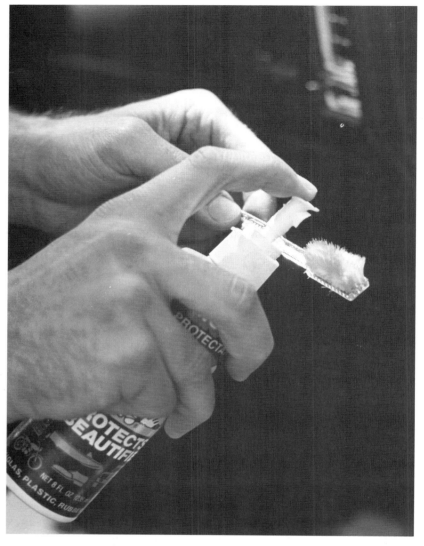

Left: Every auto detailer's equipment arsenal includes toothbrushes. The secret is in how they're used. Beyond cleaning tasks, soft bristle toothbrushes make excellent applicators for hard-to-reach places. Here, silicone protectant is sprayed onto the brush before application to interior rubber.

Remove clutch and brake pedal pads completely from your Corvette and clean them in a sink with detergent. Squeeze the pedals so the grooves open and the fine particles can be brushed out. If the detergent isn't adequate, try Acryli-Clean or lacquer thinner. Both remove gloss from rubber and clean it thoroughly. For a street-driven Corvette, these pedals will be safer because they'll be less slippery.

For a pure show Corvette, coat pedals with a silicone protectant (full strength here). Then polish with a dry rag. Make cloth "footsies" to protect the pedals from scuffing while the Corvette is driven on and off a trailer or moved on the show field. These will be slippery, so do *not* put silicone on the pedals of a street-driven Corvette. If the car sees both show and street, either skip the silicone or have a spare set of pedals.

Silicone cautions

I don't like silicone protectants for leather, and I recommend caution when using them on interior vinyl or any other interior surface. Before explaining why, let's discuss these products.

Though manufacturers won't reveal the ingredients in their formulas,

For show and street, either skip the silicone or have a spare set of pedals.

Above: Silicone products have transformed car care, but there are still right and wrong places and ways to use these. Compare different brands because formulations do vary. Armor All and Son of a Gun are milky in appearance and leave a slightly different finish than Turtle Wax's Clear Guard. Silicone protectants are most often sold in pump-spray containers, but can also be purchased in bulk. The pure silicone shown is packaged in an aerosol spray can.

it is generally known that products like Armor All and STP's Son of a Gun are water-based compounds containing silicone. It's the silicone that permits Armor All and products like it to work so effectively. Since the formulas are closely guarded secrets, it stands to reason that the different products aren't exactly the same. I've had salespeople do their best to convince me that Son of a Gun is better than Armor All, or vice versa. There may be subtle differences in application, but to me the results are similar. I tend to use whichever has a handier bottle shape and squirter. However, there are clear protectants (as contrasted to Armor All and Son of a Gun which are milky-white), like Turtle Wax's Clear Guard, which *are* different. Compared with Armor All and Son of a Gun, Clear Guard feels less slippery and appears to leave a duller sheen. For some things, I like that. For what it's worth, Clear Guard's label says it is 100% protectant and contains no water. You should experiment. You'll find you like different products for different effects.

The problem with all of these products is that they work so darn well for some things, that they get overused. There are simply places where their use is not appropriate. John Amgwert reports that he regularly used silicone protectant on the interior wood-veneer trim panels of his 1973 Corvette and ruined the veneer. He has seen other 1973 Corvettes with veneers that had never been touched and were still perfect.

I had an awful experience with Armor All several years ago. I put a heavy coating of it on the seats and door panels of a spectacular midyear Corvette before putting the car in storage for the winter. When I retrieved the car several months later, all the coated surfaces were covered with a grayish-white mold. This car and others had previously been stored, untreated with silicone, in the same garage with no problem. I phoned the manufacturer of Armor All and asked one of the chemists if the product could encourage mold or mildew. She said absolutely not *if it was used properly*. She pointed out that Armor All is water-based and that the instructions clearly state that the excess should be buffed out. If it isn't, excess moisture will remain on the surface and *that* indeed will invite mold growth.

There's a message here. When using any silicone protectant, don't make my mistake of assuming that if a little works well, a lot will work wonders. Think through what you want these products to accomplish. They're great for preventing dryness; but if you're storing where humidity is already high, they most definitely will work against you.

Remember that silicone products make surfaces slippery. That's good for minimizing wear on friction areas. But often slippery doesn't equal good. I hate the windshield suction-cup mounts that come with radar detectors and don't want to permanently deface an interior surface with some of the other mounting options. One of my solutions is to loop black photo tape to the bottom of the detector and stick it right on the dash. This works particularly well on the flat-dash 1984–1989 models. But if the dash has been treated with silicone, nothing will stick to it. Brian Hardy, a Chevrolet dealer new-car sales manager, says he hates to see Corvette trade-ins with instrument panels coated with silicone protectants. He says they never look as good as if they'd been left alone. I agree. Maybe a Corvette that was constantly exposed to sun would be the exception, but think twice before coating instrument panels, or any interior surfaces other than rubber, with silicone.

Glass

Ever notice how the glass of a Corvette show car seems to sparkle? There are several ways to achieve this. Most concours entrants have a pump-spray bottle of Windex, the type with ammonia added, in their secret bag of tricks. The secret isn't in the product, but in how it's used. Corvette people find that Windex works best as a polish, not a cleaner. In other words, get the glass clean first and then polish it with Windex. The common mistake is to clean interior glass with a few squirts of cleaner on a rag or paper towel. The dirt just gets smeared around. Liberal amounts of water must be used to flush glass clean. Use a packaged glass cleaner if you wish, but a dab of vinegar in warm water is good, too. Once glass is clean, polish with Windex. I've heard that ammonia can stain painted surfaces, but I've not had that happen with Windex. If it concerns you, Windex also has a product with vinegar added instead of ammonia.

John Amgwert reports that when he worked in the printing industry, Sparkle was the preferred product for cleaning glass. At that time, it was used somewhat exclusively in industry, but now it's in some supermarkets. John says it's the best glass cleaner he's ever used. As a cost-saving alternative, however, John suggests buying premixed windshield washer solvent in gallon jugs and transferring it to squirt bottles.

I recently noticed a glass cleaner from the makers of Rain-X. Since I love Rain-X (more on it later), I figured their glass cleaner would have to be good, so I stocked up. While I do like it for general cleaning because it doesn't dry too quickly, I don't like it for glass because it seems to streak and smear. The label claims that it makes glass water and soil repellent, so maybe it has some special ingredients that make it more difficult to use but eventually leave a better result. I called the manufacturer to gripe and was told that I was using too much. For what it's worth, the container and squirt mechanism are first rate.

Another trick you may have heard about is the newspaper routine. It's hard to believe that newspaper, with that never-drying ink that gets all over your hands and clothes, could actually be an effective glass cleaner. It can be, but again only to polish. It's not the paper that does it. It's the ink, which acts as a very fine polishing abrasive. Personally, I don't use newspaper because the ink manages to transfer to adjacent surfaces too easily. I like paper towels, especially the Scott and Coronet brands. Avoid the super-soft, plush, soak-up-big-spill brands because most are too linty. Trying to be the good citizen, I've also tried brands containing recycled paper, but so far they've been disappointing.

John Amgwert recommends another product called No-Fog for the inside window surfaces of Corvette convertibles when fogging is a problem. Moisture will still collect on the glass, but it will bead and roll off so visibility is maintained.

Bright trim

Interior brightwork isn't subjected to the elements, so Corvette show entrants often prefer not to wax these pieces to minimize wax residue on

Above: Paper towels are fine for cleaning glass, but avoid the soft, linty type. The Scott brand is excellent. Windex is best known for cleaning glass, but Corvette pros also like it for last-minute polishing of chrome and other brightwork. If ammonia is a concern, a vinegar formulation is available. Eagle One's 20/20 Perfect Vision auto glass cleaner contains neither ammonia nor vinegar. It has isopropyl alcohol and works like magic. The Rain-X glass cleaner is more difficult to use, but has extra ingredients to make glass water and soil repellent.

Right: This is the "before" photo of Corvette instruments which had never been previously cleaned.
Above: Endust is a non-wax product designed for dusting furniture without wax buildup. Its use is an effective way to prevent later dust buildup.

Scratched or cloudy plastic can usually be brought back.

adjacent surfaces. Instead, they're more likely to use a glass cleaner. (Here's a case where the Rain-X glass-cleaning product does work nicely.) Cleaning items like little bezels and radio knobs is best accomplished with a mild detergent solution, toothbrushes, and Q-tips. Once the dirt buildup is removed, glass cleaners will maintain a like-new appearance.

Instruments

Corvette instrument faces are seldom damaged or faded out, but the clear glass or plastic lenses may need cleaning or buffing. Clean glass as previously described. If a film has built up inside the lens, the instruments will have to be disassembled. After cleaning the inside of the glass, wipe it with a rag sprayed with Endust. This product makes the lint and dust adhere to the rag instead of the lens. The same holds true for plastic lenses, but plastic may require some additional steps to get it crystal clear. If plastic lenses are just dirty, try cleaning first with plain, warm water and a soft, lint-free rag. If that's not successful, try a mild detergent solution, but use very minimal pressure, as instrument plastic can easily scratch.

Scratched or cloudy plastic can usually be brought back. The trick is to remove the damage with fine abrasive and then proceed through a

Top: The glass lens from the oil pressure gauge has been cleaned in mild detergent.
Left: Once the lens has been thoroughly dried, a rag is sprayed with Endust and the lens is lightly dusted with the rag to help prevent later dust accumulation.

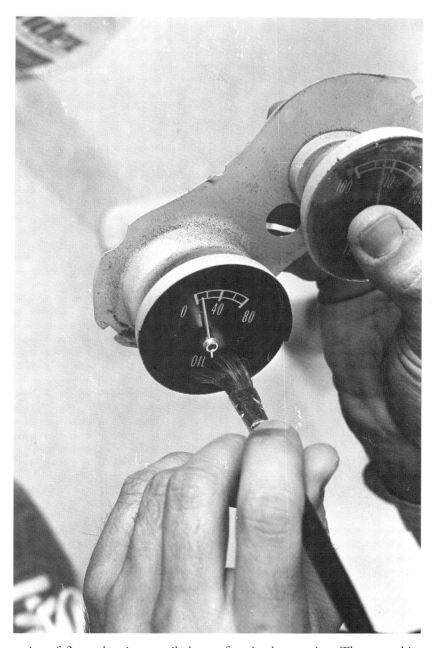

Right: A soft artist's brush is used to wipe the instrument face. No cleaners, not even water, should be applied directly to an instrument face.

Above: Jewelers rouge is a fine polish, suitable for use with a buffing wheel or by hand. Kodak's cotton gloves are designed for handling film negatives, but are also perfect for handling automobile instrument lenses because these cotton gloves are virtually lint-free.

series of finer abrasives until the surface is clear again. There are kits available to do this, such as Polysand, described in Chapter 4 in a discussion about removing scratches from convertible top windows. Another kit available at plastic suppliers is called Micro-mesh. It is a favorite in the aviation industry.

For plastic instrument lenses and other plastic parts, excellent results can be achieved by wet sanding and then polishing with jeweler's rouge on a soft buffing wheel or by hand polishing with rouge. Start with 2000-grit sandpaper, or with 600 grit dulled by rubbing two pieces of paper together. This will create a sheen on the plastic. If scratches deeper than the sheen can be seen, use fresh 600-grit paper. If that won't remove the scratches, a coarser paper and more time are needed. Using the least abrasive paper that will remove the scratches means less polishing later. Be sure to

Left: The glass lens for the oil pressure gauge has been cleaned, dusted with Endust, and replaced. Note the difference in appearance between the two instruments.

use the paper wet with light pressure in varying directions, and to keep the paper flushed with water so that the scratches left for the next step are uniform. Reverse the process so the last sanding is with the finest paper you have; then polish with rouge. Jeweler's rouge (any decent hardware store has it) is as fine an abrasive as you're likely to need for Corvette plastic polishing. Toothpaste is another excellent polish found in every home's bathroom. It is slightly more abrasive than rouge and is often adequate by itself or as a preliminary step to the rouge.

These procedures should be used only for scratched or damaged plastic surfaces. Always start with the mildest polishing or sanding technique and work into the more abrasive ones as necessary. Plastic is relatively soft, and often just a mild abrasive polish or a blended car wax product will do the job. For plastic windows, both hard and soft, John Amgwert has found that Meguiar's Sealer and Reseal Glaze works well. John says he once acquired a 1954 Corvette with a convertible top window so bad he was sure it would have to be replaced. With nothing to lose, he tried the Meguiar's Sealer and the window looked like new. Don't expect to do this

Toothpaste is an excellent polish for plastic.

Above: Air bombs for dusting negatives are available from any photo store. They're good for dusting small Corvette parts, too. Practicing first is a must, because the bombs can spray liquid propellant if held or used incorrectly. High quality brushes can be found at art supply stores. Good old paste floor wax is hard to beat for interior wood.

These beautiful wheels were actually a combination of teak and rosewood.

in ten minutes though; be prepared to spend some time. Never work a flexible piece of plastic when it is either very hot or very cold. Hot plastic can stretch; cold can crack.

For cleaning and polishing plastic, among other things, Dave Burroughs says he's found Blue Magic metal polish cream followed by Ultra Finish polish to work well. (More on these products in the chapter to follow.) Dave also likes Novus products for plastic.

Don't try to refinish the face of an instrument yourself. Companies that specialize in instruments can be found at any major Corvette show or in the advertising section of Corvette specialty magazines. (One company I've personally had good luck with is Roger's Clocks.) These companies can refurbish your instruments or exchange your damaged instruments for ones that have been rebuilt. Of course, simple repair services are available, including changing early-style clocks to quartz mechanisms. The instrument faces refurbished by these pros look really good. Still, original is original, and I don't recommend refinishing instrument faces unless it's absolutely necessary.

Hand-held air bombs sold in photo stores for dusting negatives make excellent instrument dusting devices. Hold these upright when using because they can spit propellant that could stain the instrument face. Good camel or sable hair artist's brushes from an art supply store are also handy dusting tools. As a general rule, you should not try to wash the surface of an instrument, even with plain water. But if I were at the point of having the face resurfaced, I'd probably try a soft rag dampened with plain water or glass cleaner as a last resort.

Obviously, care should be exercised around the instrument needles, and you should be careful to not demagnetize a Corvette speedometer or cable-driven tachometer by poking anything metallic into the housing.

Wood

Chevrolet used little genuine wood in Corvette interiors over the years. Wood steering wheels were optional in 1965 and 1966. Referred to as teak wheels, they were actually a combination of teak and rosewood. If you're fortunate enough to have one of these, possibly the most beautiful steering wheel ever offered in an American automobile (and now priced accordingly), care for it by cleaning with gentle soaps like Murphy Oil Soap and by using soft rags. If the finish has worn off, you can refinish is as you would any fine wood product, ultimately sealing with one of the durable polyurethane finishes available. I have an NOS teak wheel that I use as a guide, but keep in mind that a natural product like wood will vary considerably in appearance. The finish on my wheel is about midway between the gloss and satin polyurethane finishes made by companies like Zar and Minwax. I'm inclined toward satin because natural oils in the skin will increase gloss over time as the wheel is used. The wood instrument panel inlays you see in later Corvettes are aftermarket products, not factory offerings. If your Corvette has had one installed, give it the mild-soap-and-soft-rag treatment just described for cleaning steering wheels, but minimize the use of water. Windex works fine too, but spray the Windex on your cleaning rag, not directly on the wood. Wood can be waxed, but not with car wax containing abrasives. For protection, use paste furniture

wax like Trewax, liquid furniture wax like lemon-scented Pledge, or pure carnauba auto waxes without abrasives.

Starting in 1997, the floors of Corvettes have balsa wood sandwiched between plastic composites. This is a slick marriage of materials that offers a rigid, quiet, light structure. But since the balsa is completely sealed, no maintenance is required or even possible.

Above: New and beautifully refurbished seat belts are available for many Corvette models and colors as indicated by this vendor display at the annual Corvettes at Carlisle show.

Seat belts

Dave Burroughs has a nice trick for cleaning soiled Corvette seat belts. Since it is more a matter of soil being trapped between tightly woven fibers rather than actually being absorbed by the fibers, Dave removes the belts, lays them out flat, and then blasts them with the high-pressure wand at the local do-it-yourself car wash. If the soil is really stubborn, try working in some liquid dishwashing detergent by hand. Don Williams cleans seat belts with Acryli-Clean and a fingernail brush.

Is there any reason not to clean seat belts? Could be. Some Corvette belts carry a warning tag advising they shouldn't be washed. Similar cautions are often found in owner's manuals. The concern is that stitching or the belt material itself could rot with repeated wet-dry cycles. John Amgwert suggests dry cleaning as a possibility to consider. Obviously, if you're not sure of your car's history and the belts are visually suspect in any way, replacing with new ones is the safest course.

Doors and door jambs

A Corvette's door jambs are seen every time the doors are opened, but they seldom look very good. The jamb and end of the door are places

Above and right: Use gentle detergent cleaner for door jambs. For cleaning excessive adhesive or removing oil change stickers, 3M General Purpose Adhesive Cleaner works wonders. WD-40 will also thin some adhesives, and has numerous other uses as a squeak stopper, a mild lubricant, and as a penetrant for sticky mechanisms or rusty fasteners.

You may wish to leave old oil change stickers as documentation of mileage.

where a combination of road grit and latch grease accumulates. This is another area where Dawn dishwashing detergent works well. Put it on full strength and work around the rubber seals and the hinge/latch mechanisms with a toothbrush, a sponge, or your fingers. Rinse with warm water. If the rubber seals look a little shabby, spruce them up with a rag moistened with Acryli-Clean. Again, lacquer thinner for the rubber will work, but this is high-risk business because of the adjacent painted surfaces. You can relubricate the lock and latch mechanisms with one of the products made for the purpose, but don't be overly generous. Excess lubricant does no good, but it does seep out and attract dirt. If latches are working okay, you may choose not to lubricate, especially if the original grease is in place and not dried out. Dave Burroughs notes that paint overspray on the latch and starwheel (at least on midyears) was normal factory appearance. So if it's there, resist the temptation to remove it.

Go back over the rubber seals with a rubber lubricant or silicone protectant. Rub the excess off, and don't forget the door glass seals if they're rubber. Q-tips work nicely here.

If your Corvette's door has old oil-change labels, you may wish to leave them as documentation of mileage. A midyear I owned had a lube sticker from the now-defunct Pure Oil Company in its jamb. It was a neat period piece, so I just left it. But if you want to remove old stickers, use 3M General Purpose Adhesive Cleaner #08984. This is a miracle product for any adhesive removal, but it also removes silicone, wax, grease, and tar. Every home in America should have a can. I've used it to remove everything from old bumper stickers to the residue of strapping tape that held the shelves in a new refrigerator during shipping. In fact, it's a good idea to try this any time you're considering lacquer thinner because it

Above: This Amco rubber replacement mat is being sprayed with Westley's Silicone Tire Shine after cleaning. Never apply silicone to the bottoms of mats because they'll slip too much. The same caution would apply to this 1967's factory-original clear vinyl mats.

doesn't eat paint like lacquer thinner (3M does caution about use on fresh paint, however). John Amgwert says his preferred technique for removing old labels and stickers is to soak first with WD-40.

Mats

Silicone protectants like Armor All work well on rubber and vinyl floor mats. Be sure the mats are clean first (see the section on tires in the next chapter), and thin the protectant with an equal part of water. Do only the sides that face up; the mats will slip around if undersides are coated. Another silicone product you might consider for rubber or vinyl floor mats is Stoner's More Shine Less Time for Vinyl, Plastic & Rubber. This is a spray and walk away product, and really revitalizes dead-looking rubber.

The steps outlined a few paragraphs back for interior carpeting hold true for carpet-faced mats, except mats have the advantage of being easily removable. You can take advantage of the superior suction of an upright home vacuum by using it on carpet mats laid flat on the driveway or deck. Most do-it-yourself car washes have clamps to hold mats while cleaning, and you will be amazed how much dirt floats out of carpet mats cleaned this way. Repeated wet-dry cycles are hard on anything, so don't make this kind of cleaning part of routine maintenance. But I always do this for any used car I buy, followed by thorough drying and then Scotchguard protection.

Scent

There are show-car tricks for keeping a Corvette's interior smelling nice. Once interior cleaning has been completed, the scent should already

You'll be amazed how much dirt floats out of carpet mats cleaned this way.

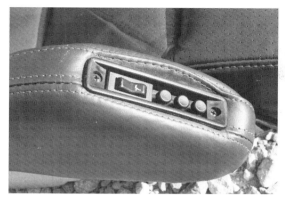

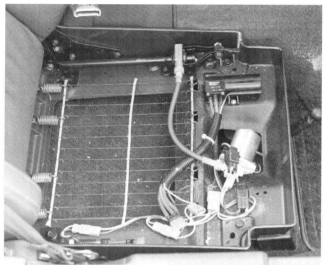

Top: The leather around this 1985's sport seat control panels started to show wear after just a few month's use. The seat control to the right is the driver's side which obviously got more wear. Other than protective covers, there really isn't a way to prevent this except by using great care when entering and exiting the vehicle.

Above and right: If interior odor is a problem, it may be necessary to treat underseat areas and other out-of-the-way places with a disinfectant like Lysol. The burlap material in the 1967 seat shown at right is more apt to hold odors. The foam construction of later models (top four photos are 1985) is less problematic for odor retention.

be pleasant because most of the products mentioned leave a nice smell behind. You can enhance this even further with a Dave Burroughs technique. First, Dave uses lemon-scented Pledge for nearly all the interior hard surfaces. Then he leaves the Pledge-coated rags and a lemon-scented air freshener inside his Corvette with the windows rolled up tight for a week. Surprisingly, this doesn't leave a phony lemon scent, just a mild, fresh smell that lasts indefinitely. This isn't something you have to repeat every few weeks; an annual treatment should suffice.

Another trick for a fresh interior in a Corvette not being used daily is an open box of baking soda. Better yet, dump the box into an aluminum pie pan for additional odor absorption. This is grandma's keep-the-refrigerator-fresh trick, but it works for car interiors too.

If your Corvette already has a stubborn, musty smell from damp storage, the closest thing to a quick fix is a spray-on odor eater. Odors result from living organisms of the fungus and mold variety, so these microcritters have to be killed. A product like Odor Exterminator from Griot's Garage will eliminate odor if it can reach the source. If not, the interior should be dismantled as far as possible. Everything should be thoroughly cleaned. Remove the seats, turn them over, and spray the bottoms with Lysol. Carpeting is often a big culprit for absorbing and holding odors. In addition to the foam carpet cleaner method mentioned earlier, there are dry types that are shaken into the carpet and vacuumed out. Cornstarch and baking soda can be used this way. The carpet must

Above: Unlike some European cars, cracked vinyl instrument panels have never been a particular problem with Corvettes, but it is still certainly possible in some climates. A light-colored sun reflector like this one will keep a Corvette's interior much cooler on sunny days.

Right: Griot's Garage sells this Odor Exterminator for eliminating interior odor. This is a superb product that will indeed get rid of odor as long as the odor's source is accessible. It is especially effective for a localized food spill or for pet urine. Just spray it on and walk away.

Far right: Pledge is the first choice of many Corvette detailers for interior vinyl because it leaves a protective, natural-looking finish.

The musty odor was replaced by a chemical one that wasn't much better.

be dry, and you need a strong vacuum. If all else fails, you may have to pull the carpet and replace the jute backing underneath, which can really hold odors. I've tried cleaning jute at the local do-it-yourself car wash, but it's awful to work with. Jute is dirt cheap and available at any upholstery shop. You can do a thorough cleaning job on the carpet itself after it is removed using the techniques already described. I once tried having a nasty Corvette carpet cleaned by a commercial dry cleaner that specialized in office carpet runners. It looked okay, but the musty odor was replaced by a chemical one that wasn't much better.

After any interior work involving moisture, be sure to let your Corvette dry thoroughly before putting it away. Nothing beats a hot, dry, breezy day. If a hot, dry, breezy day isn't to be found in your neighborhood, fire up the engine and let the heater blow full blast. Or set up a fan in the garage to circulate air through the interior. Use the Burroughs lemon-scent routine as the final step.

Chapter 4

Exterior Detailing

Beautiful paint and gleaming brightwork characterize a Corvette show car. Unfortunately, a Corvette's plastic body panels expand and contract in ways that can cause paint to crack. All 1953–1982 Corvettes were constructed with exposed body-panel joints that were filled at the factory before painting. These seams shrink and crack with age. Cracked or chipped paint, split seams, or other damage to a Corvette's body means it may have to be completely refinished before it can be a serious concours candidate. This book deals with detailing, not painting, but some understanding of painting is helpful in improving a Corvette's existing

These seams shrink and crack with age.

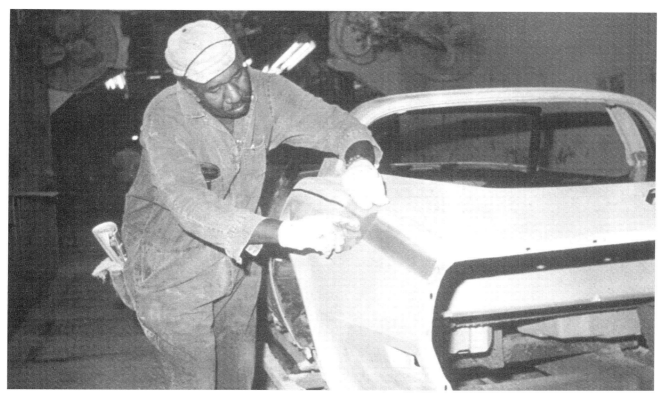

Page 66: *This 1966 Corvette has been stripped prior to repainting. The seams where body panels fit together are clearly visible.*

Above and right: *These photos show workers at the St. Louis Corvette factory filling panel seams. All 1953-1982 Corvettes had these exposed panel seams and it is common for them to show in time. Slightly visible seams are nothing to worry about unless show car quality is the goal. Starting with the 1984 model, Chevrolet designed body panels in ways that eliminated seam finishing entirely. John Amgwert photos*

finish or caring for one that has been repainted. Older Corvettes with original paint in good condition are a rare and valuable commodity. Think twice before repainting, especially until you've tried some of the detailing techniques explained on the following pages.

Cleaning

Let's start with the assumption that the subject Corvette has been street-driven and has accumulated the usual road grime. The first detailing technique is a squeaky-clean washing. Start by coating the lower half of the Corvette with kerosene, including the wheels or wheel covers and tires. Dab the kerosene onto the surface and watch soaked speckles of tar and grit dissolve and streak downward. Most Corvette frames were painted with a petroleum-based paint for which kerosene was a solvent, so don't clean the Corvette's frame members this way, and don't use so much kerosene that it runs off the body and finds its way to the frame.

Kerosene will not damage a Corvette's paint finish. Years ago, old-timers gave their cars kerosene soaks periodically to keep rust from starting behind chrome strips. Kerosene's drawback is that it is only semisoluble with water and so it doesn't rinse clean without help. A hose rinse will remove most, but a film will remain. Dave Burroughs uses his old standby, Dawn, with warm water to wash kerosene residue away. Conventional car wash products like Westley's have mild formulations designed to not strip wax. For this initial wash, use detergent. For subsequent washings of a polished or waxed Corvette, use the car wash products, a very weak detergent solution, or plain water.

The key to correct washing is to use lots of water and to make sure the wash sponge (or rag) doesn't retain grit. A common washing mistake is

Think twice before repainting.

Page 68: It's hardly a big secret, but it is important to wash from the top down because grit accumulation is heaviest toward the bottom.

Above: Car wash products don't have the cleaning muscle of household detergents, but they don't strip wax and they have excellent non-spotting additives. Prices vary. Westley's and No. 7 are moderately priced and work fine. IBIZ Car Wash is more expensive, but is designed to rejuvenate a surface that still retains some wax. Meguiar's Soft Wash Gel has outstanding sheeting action.

Above right: The transparent roof panels of this 1985 model require careful washing with lots of water, followed by gentle drying with soft towels.

trying to wash too much at one time. The surface gets scratched by fine grit held in the sponge. The scratches may be so small that individually they won't be noticed, but collectively they dull the surface. The first major cleanup isn't as critical as those following detailing, but there are still right and wrong ways to wash a Corvette.

Early evening is an ideal time to wash, but any other time will do provided the Corvette isn't in direct, hot sunlight. The sun can evaporate the water too quickly, leaving a residue that spots paint, chrome, and glass. Don Williams figures the little droplets act as mini-magnifying glasses and burn the paint a little. If you must work in the sun, first flush the painted surfaces well to cool them; then do small sections and keep rinsing both the completed and newly soaped areas.

The most important rule in Corvette washing is to wash from the top down. Wash the entire top, then all the glass area, then the hood and deck

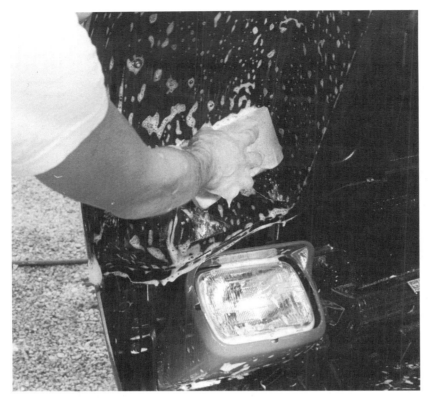

Left: The low profile tires of 1984 and later Corvettes expose the wheelwells more than earlier models. The front wheelwells of 1984-1996 models can be cleaned easily with the clam shell hood up, and this is a good time to wash the headlights as well. Do this sort of washing last, or with a separate sponge and wash bucket, because this is where the heaviest grit accumulates.

areas, then the upper fenders, then the lower fenders, then the fender lips, and then the wheels, tires, and wheelwells. It is just common sense to do it in this order because the heaviest grit accumulation is on the tires, wheels, and lower body areas. If these areas are washed first, chances are better that grit will get into the wash bucket and wind up scratching painted surfaces.

Stubborn stains on chrome can be attacked with steel wool. Several years ago, I did a little cleaning under the rear bumpers of my black '65 convertible with an SOS pad. I'd finished washing the body, but somehow a little chunk of that steel wool fell off when I dipped it into the wash bucket. It got lodged in the sponge and the next time I washed the car, I scratched the entire body without realizing it. That cost me a weekend of hand rubbing. Now, my own self-imposed rule is to never put a steel wool pad in my regular wash bucket, not even to just dampen it.

The only way around the top-down sequence is to use several buckets of washing solution and several sponges. But why bother? It is a good idea to keep an old junky sponge around just for wheelwells or particularly dirty wheels and tires. I'm thinking here of smooth wheelwells like those of 1984 and new Corvettes. For the older, rougher surfaces a long-handled, soft-bristle brush works better.

Once a Corvette is washed, dry the water off before it dries on its own. A chamois is the most common way of doing this; however, you'll not see many chamois around a Corvette concours. The thinking is that a chamois leaves streaks and, unless rinsed often, might retain grit. The preferred method is to use several old towels, preferably the lint-free variety that have been laundered umpteen times. To be perfectly candid, I've always used a chamois and still do. However, I do make several trips to

Never put a steel wool pad in your regular wash bucket.

Above: Bob Butcher, of Winners Circle International, demonstrates his company's First Pass Auto Dry Blade. It's a squeegee with a nonscratching, gum rubber blade. It is used to swish water from surfaces before using a towel or chamois for final touchup. It works best on waxed finishes that bead water well.

the kitchen sink to rinse it out, and I use old towels separately for some areas, like the transparent roof panels on my '85, lower body areas, the wheelwells, and the door jambs.

Let me tell you about a product I discovered at a Corvette show. It's called First Pass Auto Dry Blade. It was dreamed up by a fellow named Bob Butcher. Essentially it is a squeegee, but with a shape designed for auto use and with a blade made of nonscratching gum rubber. After washing, you use it to squeegee the water off before finishing with towel or chamois. For large flattish surfaces like the hoods of newer models, this thing works like gangbusters. In fact, it's almost too good. On hot, dry days you really have to hustle. If you have a helper to dry after you squeegee, you can dry a Corvette in a minute or two.

After reading the original *Secrets of Corvette Detailing* book, Bob Dienes dropped me a note describing the drying technique he uses for his 1984 Corvette: "I bought (for other reasons) a top-of-the-line Craftsman lawn blower/vacuum (hand-held, 28cc, gas powered) and I've been using it to 'blow dry' my Vette after washing. Works great. It gets the H2O out of every nook and cranny without the abrasion potential of a cloth. Any additional 'mop up' is just a pat here and there to take care of a few left over droplets. The ultra high-speed air flow actually cavitates the water

behind moldings and emblems, and washes up back there in those inaccessible places."

Reviving dead paint by sanding

Once there's a clean, dry surface with which to work, the process of bringing the finish back to life can begin. The sequence of steps required to breathe new life into a really dead finish might be to use fine sandpaper, rubbing compound, polish, and perhaps wax. If any touch-up is to be done for, say, little stone nicks in the front panels, do this after the body is thoroughly clean but before the steps just mentioned. A finish in decent shape may require only polish. One a little worse might require some rubbing compound treatment followed by polish. A poor original finish or a rough repaint may require the sanding step.

Note that I'm using the term "rubbing compound" here to include pure compound as well as heavy-duty cleaners that blend rubbing compounds with other ingredients. For now, let's also lump in "detailing clay," which is not rubbing compound at all but is used for some of the same problems. I'll describe clay in more detail later.

Many show Corvettes have all the steps, including sanding, even though paint application was anything but rough. This takes some explaining. The rule for an existing finish is to do no more than necessary. Start with the lightest paint removal technique, polishing. Work a test area to see if that is adequate. If not, go to rubbing compound. Only if the rubbing compound won't do the job should sanding be considered.

The cautions are serious here because all of these steps remove paint. Polish removes a little; rubbing compound, more; and sanding, potentially a lot. If a Corvette's finish has been around awhile, it may already be

Above: Wet-or-dry silicon carbide sandpaper, especially the 600 grit shown, has many uses in a Corvette detailer's repertoire. Some detailers dull 600 grit by rubbing two pieces together, while others prefer to keep a variety of grits for different tasks. 2000-grit paper is a favorite for sanding an existing finish, but even finer grits are made. When very fine grits are used, try adding a little detergent to the water. This keeps the paper from loading.

All of these steps remove paint.

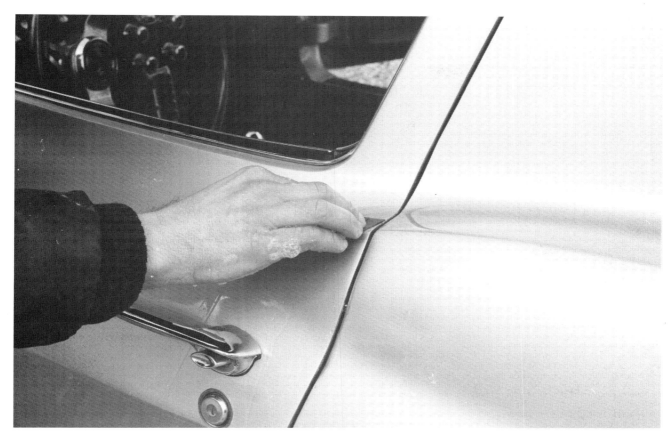

Above: Wet sanding finish coats is common when repainting Corvettes, but should be attempted only with great caution when detailing an existing finish because even the finest grades of paper can remove considerable amounts of paint. In either case, fold sandpaper a couple of layers think to avoid grooving when surfaces require a bare fingers sanding technique.

getting thin. A little sanding and rubbing, and the primer shows through.

A number of years ago, Bill Munzer and Don Williams "built" a 1963 Corvette show car with a finish that approached perfection. At the time I wrote the following comments about the importance of sanding to achieve a show-car finish.

"Everyone knows that body refinishing requires a great deal of sanding. What some people don't know is that the most important paint step of all is the last one, the sanding of the final top coat.

"You'll have to search a long way to find a body shop that sands the final top coat before polishing. They'll look at you like you're half crazy if you request it. The argument you'll get is that sanding removes too much paint. The real reason is that too much time is required.

"Bill Munzer's and most winning show cars have had this last crucial sanding step. Regardless of how well the final paint coat is applied, there will exist some small degree of texturing in the paint surface. Think of it as a series of microscopic peaks and valleys. When polishing by hand or even a power buffer, the peaks are smoothed down, but the valleys get deepened a little at the same time. This is due to the flexibility of the polishing cloth or buffer pad. No matter how long you polish, the surface will never be dead flat.

"By wet sanding first with a well-worn 600-grit sandpaper, backed with a hard rubber block, the surface can be trued before polishing.

"The one word of caution is that sanding does indeed remove paint and this must be done with extreme care. As the surface is being sanded, the portions touched by the paper will take on a dull sheen. The untouched

low spots will stay bright and shiny. It's a good idea to leave just a trace of the shiny specs as a depth guide. If you sand until nothing is left but the sheen, you may go too deep."

When I wrote that over two decades ago, 600 grit was the finest grade of wet-dry sandpaper commonly available. Now 2000 grit is easy to find and even finer grits are made. Tom Tucker and Don Williams both have tried finer-grit papers and have reverted to 600 grit. Don swears the finer grit makes deeper scratches. It doesn't sand as clean, so he figures it holds particles of paint that cut deeper than the paper's abrasive. Tom Tucker says he never throws a piece of 600 grit away. He keeps tossing them in an old bucket. When he needs very fine paper, he roots through the bucket until he finds just the right piece. Remember that both Tom and Don are looking at this from a painter's perspective. Later you'll hear some strong praise for 2000 grit.

Also, the statement that practically no body shops do this isn't true today. The boom in concours events during the past two decades, especially Corvette concours, has led many high-quality shops to follow this exact procedure.

There are some other important points to be made about Corvette show paint. For example, when Don Williams sprays a Corvette, he puts double coats on all the character lines and peaks. This is because when you're sanding, rubbing, and polishing, these areas will get more abrasion no matter how careful you are. With a Corvette that's not been painted this way, one must be very cautious to not sand or rub through these areas.

The purpose of wet-sanding the finish coat is to smooth the finish to a dead-flat surface. Skipping the sanding step won't result in a car with any less gloss, just with less of that smoothness characteristic of show Corvettes.

Don't confuse this sanding with what Corvette enthusiasts call "blocking." Blocking is the removal of natural waves in the fiberglass. It's less popular today than in years past because of the desire for strict originality. The sanding discussed in this section does use small hand-

Above: Wet sanding is best accomplished with a hard rubber block backing the sandpaper. This works for flat surfaces, but other techniques are required for the many curved surfaces found on every Corvette body style.

Leave just a trace of the shiny specs as a depth guide.

Pause and consider the possibility of salvaging original paint, regardless of its condition.

held blocks, but it's not the same as blocking, which requires much larger tools. Blocking is passé in the Corvette world today.

If you're sanding a paint coat, use plenty of water to keep the sandpaper clean. Milt Antonick, Don Williams, and Tom Tucker, enthusiasts who do this often, all suggest adding a little detergent to the sanding water. It works like magic, keeping the paper from loading by flushing grit from the surface during sanding.

If you know there is plenty of paint to work with, you can use a power buffer after the sanding step to get the bulk of the work done, followed by hand polishing to get the power buffer marks. But with an existing finish, using a power buffer is extremely risky. Going over a complete Corvette that isn't a recent repaint with a power buffer almost guarantees that some surface will have the paint buzzed off down to primer or that a bit of chrome plating will be knocked off the edge of a Corvette script or emblem. If it's used just for flat areas, avoiding the peaks and emblems, it's less dangerous. But even then, it's easy to remove too much paint. I've been experimenting with a small Black & Decker orbital polisher lately. It isn't aggressive at all, and is quite easy to control.

Working strictly by hand does take time. For me though, slowly rubbing a Corvette's finish back to life by hand, up close where you can see it happening, is pure joy. Maybe I'm nuts, but for me this is the best part of Corvette detailing.

When a Corvette's paint is thin, chipped, and generally dulled by age, it is certainly tempting to just strip it and start over. For many years, that seemed to be the preferred route. The demands of show judging and the prestige of achieving a Bloomington Gold, rather than Silver, or an NCRS Top Flight all conspired to cause a lot of Corvettes with decent original paint to lose that paint. It's a shame, because regardless of the care taken, original paint can never be perfectly duplicated. We've lost a lot of history here. That's why you should at least pause and consider the possibility of salvaging original paint, regardless of its condition.

In this spirit, let me describe one of my recent purchases. I'd been on the trail of a particular midyear convertible for several years. The car had been purchased new by a young doctor just out of med school and then sold privately in the early eighties to the lady who still owned it. What appealed to me was that this Corvette had been in California all its life, so the chassis was spotless. Also, the paperwork trail was complete, including the window sticker. The car was for sale, then it wasn't. Then it was, then it wasn't. In situations like these, it pays to be patient. When someone has owned a Corvette for many years, selling is a difficult emotional decision. So I waited and eventually purchased the car.

This car was anything but pristine. The body had mostly original paint (Sunfire Yellow), was very, very dull. There was little actual fiberglass damage, but the paint was badly chipped across the nose from road debris and down each side from parking lot dings. The normal body seams were showing, but they weren't openly cracked. Light colors are forgiving in highlighting seams anyway. I've seen so many flawlessly restored Corvettes at shows, they're almost commonplace. I wanted to try salvaging the original paint on this car even if the final result wasn't perfect. I entrusted the job to a long-time Corvette ace, Steve Ward.

Steve has a one-man shop in Anderson, California, and is one of those people who knows classic Corvettes like the back of his hand. He is a master at body repair that duplicates factory technique and appearance. My Corvette needed a little of this, but for the purposes of this text, I want to describe how he handled the chips and saved the original paint.

Steve started by acquiring a little NOS (new-old-stock) Sunfire Yellow lacquer. He shined up a small patch of paint and then tinted the paint by adding a little white (with age, paint will change shade slightly). Steve carefully built up paint in the chipped areas by dabbing with a small brush until the paint filled the chip above the surrounding surface. Then he filed the new paint down flush with an ingenious, self-designed tool, nothing more than a 1-inch section of a flat file glued into a small wood holder. At this point, the chips were filled, but the original paint was mostly untouched. Next, he sanded the entire car with 2000-grit paper. Steve doesn't agree with using 600 grit or detergent as our other pros prefer. Steve uses 2000 grit with plain water. He says it simply removes the least paint. The surface left by the 2000 grit was so smooth, just polishing with fine polishing compound finished the job. Steve used an orbital power buffer, but only for the open flat areas. For everything else, he polished by hand. Believe me, the transformation was incredible. All things considered, it would have cost little more to have just repainted the car. But how many real survivors are left?

How many real survivors are left?

With all this glorification of sanding, let me interject some additional cautions. The paper should be kept flat. Accomplish this by backing it with something other than fingers. Fingers cause uneven pressure and grooves. The standard hard rubber block available at any auto paint jobber and most hardware stores is good, but won't follow many of the Corvette's compound body forms. For some surfaces, it may be necessary to use a sanding device with a flexible foam backing. John Amgwert wraps sandpaper around small sections of radiator hose, heater hose, etc. But let's face it, in some areas paper and fingers will be the only feasible combination. Minimize the grooving danger by folding the sandpaper over a few times and by continually changing the sanding direction.

When the Corvette plant moved from St. Louis to Bowling Green, a new paint process involving clear top coats began to be used. Although Corvette restorers often like to duplicate the factory's original paints and primers when repainting an older Corvette, using clear top coats is nothing new to show Corvettes or other show cars. If I were restoring an older Corvette that wasn't clear-coated by the factory, I wouldn't use clear. But I'll admit that some of the best paint jobs I've seen have been cleared. For show-car appearance, Tom Tucker follows the color coats with several coats of a 15% color, 85% clear mixture. This is allowed to cure for a week or so, then wet sanded. Then pure clear goes on. This is sanded, rubbed, and polished. Show-car painters put plenty of clear on, knowing they'll be sanding some off. I'm told that GM puts enough clear on its production cars to permit a little sanding, but you have to be very cautious because if the clear is sanded or rubbed through, the difference in finish will be noticeable. If it happens, the only real remedy is to apply a new clear coat.

Show-car painters put on plenty of clear, knowing they'll be sanding some off.

The trend for manufacturers to use clear coat paint processes is another reason that routine power buffing, a la detailing shops, is risky business.

Top and right: *Don't try to touch up small chips with a big brush, or with thick paint. Very small brushes are available at artist supply stores. A local paint jobber can mix a pint of nearly any Corvette color so that small batches of touch up paint can be thinned to the proper consistency when needed.*

Above: *Though the packaging has changed, Dupont 606S rubbing compound has been around for decades. It is ideal for hand rubbing Corvette lacquer finishes. Used properly, fine compounds like this one will remove oxidation, stains, and fine abrasion marks perfectly. A much broader range of specialized rubbing compounds is available from professional auto paint jobbers as compared to general auto stores.*

On the other hand, Tom Tucker points out that one reason for the clear is to prevent the color coats from oxidizing, so these finishes theoretically will need less buffing of any kind.

Rubbing compound

Sanding is normally followed by some grade of rubbing compound. If you've skipped sanding, rubbing compound could be the first step. Rubbing compound comes in different formulations. Applied by a power buffer, "machine" compound can remove paint in a hurry. But fine rubbing compound applied by hand doesn't take nearly as much paint off as either sanding or machine rubbing. Still, it is a paint removal process and the same cautions apply. For Corvette finishes just being freshened, it will be necessary to use the compound only in selected areas. Stubborn stains can be taken out with rubbing compound, as well as scratched areas around door handles and locks. Something milder will usually get rid of dried bugs on the front-end surfaces, but if they've baked on there for a long time, they may have to be rubbed out with compound.

Buy fine rubbing compound for hand application at an auto paint jobber. You'll have to purchase a larger quantity than you'll need, but it doesn't spoil, it will eventually be used, and the price will be much more reasonable. A favorite of mine is Dupont #606S Polishing Compound, but similar products are available from all major automotive paint manufacturers. Rubbing compound with very fine abrasive is often called "polishing" compound, but don't confuse this with conventional polish, a fine white formula for hand application. It can be thinned with water to a smooth-paste consistency. Consider transferring some from the can to a squeeze bottle, premixed with water.

With practice you'll develop a good hand motion for the finish being worked. An important trick with rubbing compound is to apply considerable pressure initially and then lighten the pressure as the compound starts to dry. You don't just put compound on, let it dry, and then wipe it off like polish or wax. This is work. Keep rubbing the compound as it dries until it disappears. If you lighten the pressure as the compound dries, the finished section will be bright and shiny. A little compound will be left behind though, so some people like to give their Corvette another washing before polishing.

Where does detailing clay fit into this picture? Detailing clay is a grippy, nonabrasive material that is rubbed over painted finishes to remove surface contaminants. Clay has been in use by detailing pros, body shops, and car dealers for years, but wasn't actively marketed to the consumer market until the mid-1990s. Clay will not help with any defect that is etched into the paint. Its effectiveness is limited to sap, acid rain, tar, overspray, fallout—things on top of, not *in*, the paint. The beauty of clay is that it is nonabrasive, so no paint is removed.

To use clay, massage it into a pancake shape and rub over a surface that has been sprayed with a special lubricant. Sellers of clays also sell the lubricants. As it is used, reshape the clay to expose fresh surfaces. For certain surface problems, clay is a wonderful tool. It creates a smooth, slick surface for polishing or waxing. Detailing clays are not cheap, and if you drop a clay on the ground, it has to be discarded. Simply refolding it won't suffice. Meguiar's has separate clay products aimed at consumer and professional markets. Consumer clays are also available from Mother's, Griot's Garage, and Auto Wax.

Top: *The use of a power buffing wheel is fine as part of a Corvette's repainting process, but it's extremely risky otherwise. Even when used to apply wax or polish, power buffers remove too much material, especially from fender peaks, character lines, panel edges, and emblems. Don't make use of a power buffer as part of your routine Corvette detailing.*
Above: *Detailing clay—the one shown is from Meguiar's—doesn't remove paint at all. Used with a lubricant, it removes sap, tar, acid rain, paint overspray, or other things on, not in, the paint.*

Polishing and waxing

In the earlier edition of this book, polishing and waxing were treated as separate subjects. They're not the same, but there is considerable overlap,

The elements start taking their toll when the wax barrier has sacrificed itself away.

and I think it clearer to cover them simultaneously.

There are two fundamental decisions. First is when to polish and when to wax. Second is which products work best and how to use them.

To make the first decision, you need to know the difference between polish and wax, and what each does. In a nutshell, polish cleans and shines the surface. A slick surface is protected in the sense that contaminants have trouble sticking, but a true polish doesn't actually leave a protective coating behind. For this reason, you can polish your car scores of times without buildup of the polish. A true wax, on the other hand, neither cleans nor polishes, but does leave a protective, sacrificial coating behind. It is sacrificial in that it sacrifices itself to the elements. When the wax barrier has sacrificed itself away, that's when the elements start taking their toll on the finish itself.

So wouldn't you always want wax protection? Generally yes, but an exception is a Corvette used only for show. Nearly all auto waxes have a carnauba wax base. Most carnauba in its natural state is yellow, so that's why unless other color has been added, carnauba-based car wax is almost always a shade of yellow. Since wax does leave a thin film behind, it is possible to yellow a finish with enough coats. For most of us in real life who use our cars even sparingly, this is never going to happen. But if I had a Corvette that was only used for show, I'd use pure polish and not use wax. You don't need wax's protection from the elements, and you could polish it to your heart's content and never worry about buildup.

There are products, however, that completely contradict what I've just said. Some people say you should never wax any car. There are wax manufacturers who say once you've got good wax protection on a street or show car, you don't need to keep waxing because if you use their special wash products, the wax will be activated for months. I'll explain all these nuances as I explain several products and the results you can expect.

When I was sixteen, I repainted my first car, a 1954 Studebaker coupe. I did it myself in my parent's gravel driveway with a dinky Sears compressor and Binks gun. The car had a decent original black finish, but at the time I was crazy about 1963 Corvette Daytona Blue, so I changed the color to that. I used nitrocellulose lacquer, and despite a little grit and a few gnats, it came out terrific. Other than advice from guys at the paint store, no one was around to help. What I learned rubbing and polishing and eventually waxing that paint "the old-fashioned way" has stayed with me. Not long after the Stude, I bought a used Daytona Blue '63 Corvette, the first of many. For years, I got by with three products for maintaining my Corvettes' finishes: Dupont's finest-grit hand-polishing compound, Dupont No 7 polish, and a pure paste wax called Classic.

Today, things are more complicated. Sometimes I still follow a similar three-step process, but now there is a plethora of products from which to choose, and some are really good. The downside of my compound-polish-wax routine was the work. Pure wax doesn't contain abrasive, so if the car had been exposed at all, it was necessary to at least repeat the polishing step. If you do polish before waxing, by the way, you'll be amazed at how long a container of wax lasts.

Anyway, over the years manufacturers have gone to great lengths to make all this easier. Their most common solution is a single product that does all the cleaning, polishing, and waxing in one step. This takes the form of a wax with some cleaning and polishing agents mixed in. Turtle Wax, which claims to be the world's best-selling auto wax, fits this category along with other well-knowns like Raindance. My feeling about products in this general category is that they do very well in ease of use and cleaning, but fall short for finish and protection. (I'm speaking here of "entry level" products. There has been a tremendous influx of premium car care products into the market in recent years, and companies like Turtle Wax have introduced new, more expensive lines.) This isn't to say I never use them. A few years ago, I had a red car (not a Corvette) with a finish that dulled after a month no matter what I put on it. This car was ten years old when I bought it and probably had never seen a bit of polish or wax, so no doubt the finish had suffered permanent damage. But it would temporarily shine up, so I used Turtle Wax because it was quick and easy.

Above: Companies like Turtle Wax have entered the premium car-care-product wars with upgraded formulations. The Emerald Series from Turtle Wax is a carnauba wax with cleaner. Ultra Shield is a polish with a particularly strong following among aircraft enthusiasts.

There's another relatively new category of products which are designed to be used without first washing the car. You spritz these on a dirty (not filthy) car and then wipe off. If this makes you cringe, you're not alone, but keep an open mind. I was talked into trying some of this stuff and the results were impressive. Products in this category include Meguiar's Quik Detailer, IBIZ Waterless Wash & Wax Protectant, Ultra Mist from Ultra Finish Products, and Dri Wash 'n Guard from Enviro-Tech International.

In the catchall category, I'll also describe some products that are neither polish nor wax but can be very useful, and I'll throw in some unorthodox tips and techniques.

Let's start with some polishes. Dave Burroughs grew up around airplanes, and airplane people like a polish called Astro Shield. It was Dave's favorite for many years. At the time this book's first edition was written, Dave had found something he liked better, actually the combination of two products used together. The first was Blue Magic Metal Polish Cream. The second was Ultra Finish. Dave said the cream was great for chrome, but he saw it demonstrated on paint and couldn't believe how well it worked on black followed by the Ultra Finish. These products are relatively expensive, and Dave wasn't sure how well they protected, but they did get his vote for visual impact.

Above: The manufacturer of Ultra Finish polish recommends the use of Blue Magic Metal Polish Cream in combination with Ultra Finish. The Blue Magic can be used between a fine sanding and Ultra Finish, or as just a precleaner to Ultra Finish.

Dave was so impressed with the combination of Blue Magic Metal Polish Cream and Ultra Finish that I decided to get some and try them myself, and to get some insight from the source. Richard Romberg, the owner of Ultra Finish Products, told me that Ultra Finish is a proprietary product of his company. He also sells a lot of Blue Magic Metal Polish Cream, but the polishing cream is a product of Blue Magic, Inc. Seems Richard was intrigued with Blue Magic's cream because it used the same abrasive as that used in the optical industry to polish plastic eyeglass lenses. After experimenting, he realized it would be an ideal product to use between rubbing compound or fine sanding and Ultra Finish, or simply as a cleaner before Ultra Finish. For a dull finish, Richard recommends (and has demonstrated countless times at Corvette shows) sanding with 2000-grit sandpaper (dry!), followed by the Blue Magic, followed by Ultra Finish. He mentioned that because the carrier in Blue Magic's cream tends to dry out when used on paint, a little Ultra Finish can be added to the rag during this step. Or just mix Ultra Finish with the Blue Magic to make a

80

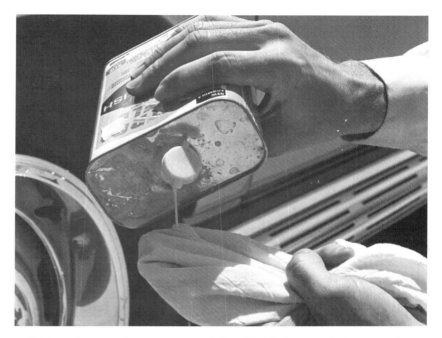

Above: Liquid Glass is a unique carbon-based polish that some Corvette enthusiasts swear by.
Above right: Regardless of your polish choice, it's best to pour polish on the polish rag, not directly on the paint surface.

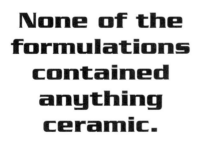

polishing slurry before you start. Ultra Finish is one of those products well known in Corvette show circles, but you're not likely to find it in your local hardware or auto parts store. Like Dave Burroughs, most customers see it demonstrated and then purchase it at a show or directly by mail order.

Another polish not commonly available but known in Corvette circles is Liquid Glass. Shortly after this book's first edition was published, Captain L. W. Reimer Jr. wrote me wondering why Liquid Glass was omitted. Here's what he said: "Notice you made no mention at all of a polish that most Vette Nuts in my area swear by, Liquid Glass Polish. It's a ceramic, not a silicone or wax, and after the first two-coat application, can have any number of coats applied with no buildup or yellowing. I, for one, have used it since after the 90-day new paint drying time suggested and had remarkable results. Have you had any bad result info on this polish and therefore kept it from being mentioned as an alternative in your book?"

At the time of this book's first edition, I hadn't used Liquid Glass and none of the contributors mentioned it, so that's why it wasn't included. Captain Reimer's comments were unsolicited and obviously reflect a satisfied customer, but he wrote those words several years ago. The list of ingredients on my can of Liquid Glass didn't include anything that sounded ceramic so I did some checking. John Heywang, the inventor of Liquid Glass and owner of the company that sells it, told me that Liquid Glass was first introduced in 1984. Since then it has been reformulated three times due to changes in new-car painting processes. None of the formulations has ever contained anything ceramic (probably a misunderstanding related to the "glass" in its name). Liquid Glass has a unique carbon-based formula, according to Mr. Heywang, who is an avid automobile collector. In addition to polish, Liquid Glass also has a pre-cleaner, a wash concentrate, a protectant, and a cleaner. Captain Reimer's positive experience and those of his Corvette cohorts speak well for Liquid Glass, so this is a niche product that could become your favorite.

None of the formulations contained anything ceramic.

Speaking of favorite, now I'll tell you mine. I use lots of different polishes and waxes, but what I reach for first is IBIZ Car Wax, a product of IBIZ Inc. If I had to clear everything off the shelf except one, this would be it. I saw Robert Nathan demo this at the Corvettes at Carlisle show several years ago. I am by nature a terrible skeptic. The more impressive a demonstration, the less likely I'll buy. But I couldn't help but admire Mr. Nathan's work ethic. Nobody works harder and longer at showing what his products will do. And he owns the company! So I gave it a try and it has become my overall favorite.

I phoned Robert for a little insight. He told me that his grandfather and great uncle started the company nearly a hundred years ago. The IBIZ Car Wax product I like is made from montan wax, which is a 25 to 58-million-year-old, fossilized carnauba. It is mined in Germany and Austria, heated to 182°F to extrude the wax from the fossil, and then filtered and cleaned. IBIZ has its own manufacturing facility.

Next, I asked Robert to describe the steps he would recommend for restoring a Corvette's finish and protecting it. I specified a finish that was a little tired and dull, but not shot. Robert described the IBIZ "system." Start by washing with IBIZ Car Wash, which has very little suds. Follow this with IBIZ Waterless Wash & Wax Protectant. Do a 2 foot-square section at a time. Spray it wet; wipe it off wet. Robert likens this to a spit shine or a facial at the beauty salon. He says it will penetrate right into the microscopic pores of the paint and will dissolve, loosen, and thin out any oxidation, grease, grime, or dirt that is beneath the surface of a clearcoat or non-clear-coat paint. This product has enough wax in it to protect for thirty days. But if you follow it with the IBIZ Car Wax, this gives

It's like a spit shine or a facial at the beauty salon.

Page 82: Robert Nathan, president of IBIZ Inc., is shown demonstrating IBIZ Car Wax and IBIZ Waterless Wash & Wax Protectant at the annual Corvettes at Carlisle show. **Right:** *IBIZ makes numerous car care products, but these are two of its most popular. IBIZ Car Wax is made from montan wax, a fossilized carnauba mined in Germany and Austria. The IBIZ Waterless Wash & Wax Protectant puts less actual wax on the surface than IBIZ Car Wax, but is very easy and quick to use. It is excellent as a pre-wax prep, or for easy maintenance of a previously waxed finish.*

To avoid streaking, do not use fabric softener when buffing towels are washed.

about a seven-month protection. Washing with IBIZ Car Wash will maintain the finish. It doesn't lay new wax down, but it has a "predispersed emulsion" of wax particulates that refresh wax still on the paint. Robert says you'll think you've just spent five hours detailing the finish.

For years, I used Dupont's powdered car wash. Now I mostly use Westley's liquid. If you're used to a conventional car wash product with lots of suds, you'll immediately notice that IBIZ's product is very different because there is almost no sudsing action. Suds may not clean any better, but since I often wash cars late in the evening in low light, suds at least show me where I've washed. But let me describe one non-Corvette instance where IBIZ Car Wash really worked.

My black MR2 had a nice IBIZ wax job but had to sit outside in a repair shop's gravel holding yard for a month waiting for an ABS part. When I got it back, it looked pretty grim. When blasted with the hose, there was no sheeting action. Then I washed with IBIZ Car Wash, and sure enough, the surface beaded water. Once I dried it off, it looked great. At this point I tried the IBIZ Waterless Wash & Wax Protectant on one panel. It worked as advertised. But since the IBIZ Wax is so easy to use, especially when the paint is in good shape, I just rewaxed the whole car in about an hour.

I mentioned to Robert Nathan that I used old towels for applying polish and wax and for buffing. I discard the applicator towels because I don't want the wax in my septic system, but wash the buffing towels for use again. Robert advised not using fabric softener, just detergent to wash towels to avoid streaking. He sells and recommends an applicator with cotton on one side and foam on the other. The foam has more grip and works better on oxidized surfaces; the cotton is better for surfaces in good shape.

Now on to some other products you should know about. I owned a BMW for a short while years ago, but never dropped my subscription to

the BMW club magazine, *Roundel*, which is really well done and a joy to browse through. BMW people seem to agree that a product called Zymöl is God's gift to paint, because a high percentage of cars for sale by individuals tout its use as one justification for a hefty asking price. On a separate note, an article done by *British Car Magazine* back in 1992 compared five auto waxes. While the things I relate to you about my experiences and those of contributors tend to be anecdotal, *British Car* did some rigorous testing that bordered on being scientific. Without getting into the details, suffice to say that Zymöl was ranked best over Auto Glym, Eagle One, Meguiar's, and Turtle Wax.

Zymöl has a number of products. I've been using Zymöl HD-Cleanse, a pre-wax cleaner, and Zymöl Auto Polish for about two years. They are both excellent products, but they are considerably more expensive than some good alternatives. Like virtually every other product discussed in this text, there are situations where I think nothing works better, but other times when I can't say that. To be fair, I have not used all the company's products. Some of Zymöl's waxes are unbelievably expensive. If cost is no object, they'll create and custom-blend products for specific automobiles! What is most intriguing about Zymöl's products is that they claim to be completely plant-based (does FD&C Blue come from plants?). Instead of the petroleum distillates you see on the ingredient lists of competing products, Zymöl has plant oils like coconut, pineapple, banana, cinnamon bark and apricot. The wax products have yellow or white Brazilian carnauba. Zymöl sells applicators, but recommends bare hands as the best applicators. The Zymöl I've used feels and smells great, better than most hand lotions. The whole garage smells good! Well, almost.

Corvette people are more down-to-earth than the BMW bunch, so maybe Zymöl strikes Corvetters as a little snooty. On the other hand, if convinced a product was better, the Corvette folks I know would spend the extra money in a heartbeat. Zymöl sends an "Owner's Manual" describing its products and their use at no cost. A nice touch is that the

Zymöl has plant oils like coconut, pineapple, banana, cinnamon bark, and apricot.

Above: *Meguiar's is well represented at major auto shows around the country. This company, in business since 1901, sells over 200 car care products. Nothing beats discussing a paint problem face to face with a company's knowledgable representative, and that is one advantage of shopping at shows for your wax and polish needs.*

Meguiar's offers good advice by phone or on its web site.

ingredients of each product are listed, even including the percentages of carnauba contained.

Another Zymöl endorsement comes from Dave Burroughs. On an old but sound lacquer finish, Dave found that Zymöl HD-Cleanse was top-notch. He used it on a 1967 L88's Rally Red original paint, followed by a nonabrasive carnauba wax (Eagle One), and says he's never seen a better result.

A brand that is very familiar in Corvette circles is Meguiar's. This is a family-owned business that started formulating polishes in 1901. The company currently sells over 200 products, and I don't have a single Corvette acquaintance who doesn't use at least one. The company manufactures in its own facility, and in addition to products carrying the Meguiar's name, it also formulates and packages for others. For example, next time you visit your GM dealer parts department, look at the wax and polish products. Though they have GM labels, Meguiar's is identified as the manufacturer.

Meguiar's is consumer-oriented. Good advice is available by phone and on its web site. You can even describe your vehicle by mail or fax and receive a customized evaluation including recommended products and techniques.

Meguiar's vast array of products is both a blessing and a curse. If you once bought a Meguiar's product at a discount store and didn't think it that great, you must realize that Meguiar's aims products at the entire market spectrum (the *British Car* magazine article I mentioned earlier that favored Zymöl, for example, used Meguiar's least expensive products, which cost about one-tenth as much as Zymöl, hardly an objective test). Meguiar's has lines for the price-conscious low end and for the true professional, and some in between. Meguiar's constantly tweaks its product lineup, so any review of its product lines is bound to be somewhat out of date. Just the same, here's a Meguiar's product overview.

Mirror Glaze is Meguiar's professional line, and it includes a wide range of cleaners, polishes, waxes, glazes, overspray clay, sandpaper in grits to 2000, swirl remover, sealants, washes, and specific products for vinyl, rubber, wheels, metal and plastic. You get the picture. Within the Mirror Glaze group is the Medallion line, which is a top-of-the-market consumer product. This line currently includes Premium Paint Cleaner, Premium Paint Protection, and Premium Leather Care.

Meguiar's least expensive line is generally packaged in maroon containers and includes a basic cleaner/wax, a Deep Crystal System polish and a wax, a nonwax Quick Detailer mist and wipe product, and a Clay Detailer.

Positioned between this group and the professional Mirror Glaze products is the newer Gold Class lineup, which includes paste and liquid waxes, wash, leather cleaner/conditioner, and a swirl reducer. Gold Class liquid wax costs about twice as much as Deep Crystal wax. Medallion Premium Paint Protection costs about twice as much as Gold Class wax.

The less expensive Meguiar's products tend to be more user friendly. That is, they're easy to use with little experience or expertise. In preparation for writing this text, I purchased a whole range of Meguiar's to sample, eventually confirming what I expected. The Gold Class products are a very good compromise of cost and ease of use, but you just can't beat the Mirror Glaze line. If your budget can stand it, buy every Mirror Glaze product available in 16-ounce containers, and you'll be set. For the two wash choices, Car Wash & Conditioner and Soft Wash Gel, I prefer the gel for its terrific sheeting action.

Andy Roderick's garage was one of ten "Garage Mahals" selected by *Car & Driver* for one of the "ten best" issues. The first time I visited Andy's place, I couldn't get over the appearance of his bright red Corvette convertible. It looked like the poster car for a detailing promotion. Andy assured me it always looked that way, so I wanted to know how he did it. Andy usually spends a little time each day detailing, but he seldom washes his Corvette first. If there's a lot of grit, he'll wash, but more often he just gently wipes the car down with a damp towel to remove dirt. Now and then, Andy uses a little Meguiar's Quick Detailer and a little Armor All,

Above: Meguiar's sells a terrific range of car care products aimed at the entire market spectrum from amateur to professional. "Mirror Glaze" designates the professional series and includes such products as Medallion Premium Paint Cleaner and Premium Paint Protection. The Mirror Glaze line also includes the numbered series—#9 Swirl Remover and #40 Vinyl & Rubber Cleaner/Conditioner shown here. The Gold Class line is aimed at an upscale customer. Quick Detailer and Cleaner-Wax are mass-market products, available almost everywhere.

Above: Griot's Garage is a mail order company selling all sorts of premium automobile products including its own line of polishes and waxes. Shown here are Griot's Fine Hand Polish and Best of Show Wax. DRI WASH 'n GUARD is a waterless car wash and protective glaze. Cotton diapers make excellent polishing cloths because they are nearly lintless. Buy them from a diaper service if you can still locate one, or from auto wax companies. The package shown is available from IBIZ, Inc.

but his product of choice is DRI WASH 'n GUARD from a multi-level marketing sales company called Enviro-Tech International. Enviro-Tech specializes in waterless and water-saving technologies, and Andy says this product, a "waterless car wash and protective glaze," is unlike anything he's ever used. It's also quite expensive.

Andy mentioned to me that he'd tried detailing products from Griot's Garage, a high-line mail-order company, but wasn't impressed. I have used Griot's polishes and waxes and found them to be very good, but I question their cost. Griot's product line is generally very high quality and very expensive and seems aimed at the Ferrari-Porsche end of the market. Having said that, hardly a month goes by that I don't order something from Griot's. The company's throwaway latex gloves, for example, are the best I've ever found. There are any number of handy items like itsy-bitsy touch-up brushes, ratcheting lights, extendable hood props, portable air tanks, wall mounts for tires, and a creeper comfortable enough to sleep on. The selection is terrific.

All the products mentioned include detailed instructions for their uses, but let's talk about technique for a moment. Some companies either include applicator pads with their products or sell them separately. I admit they work great for a while, but I think they lose effectiveness as they load up. Bill Munzer orders well-used and -laundered cotton diapers from a local service for final polishing of his show Corvettes. They're nearly lintless, and there's nothing softer except maybe cotton balls. He uses those, too. Right before judging, Bill puts a mist coat of Windex on all painted surfaces, one area at a time and then wipes down with a diaper. He says it leaves a beautiful shine with no lint or streaks. He uses a soft, pure bristle brush around emblems and body seams.

Get this. Dave Burroughs polishes with paper towels. He uses the soft kind, like Bounty. He folds a single sheet into quarters, crumples it with a damp hand and then applies the polish. He says he's tried everything else and nothing works better. He thinks they work so well because they don't soak up a lot of polish. Only a little polish is needed, and most of it goes onto the surface. As soon as a towel is dirty, he pitches it and gets another. It certainly is an inexpensive solution. Dave applies nonabrasive carnauba wax with his bare hands. He says he got the idea from watching shoe shine pros. The beauty of this is that hands won't scratch, there's no lint, and you can build up just the right heat to dissolve the wax. Dave rubs in a fore and aft motion, not circular. He rubs until the wax is gone, and he does not touch the waxed surface with a buffing cloth.

Milt Antonick reports there's a giant roll of cheesecloth in the model shop near his design studio. What's needed is unrolled and snipped off. Cheesecloth is expensive, but if you can obtain it in bulk from an industrial supplier, a roll of it in the garage would certainly be handy.

Nothing looks worse on a newly freshened Corvette than globs of dried polish or wax showing in cracks and crevices. The first time though, the necessary time will have to be spent polishing these areas to get the excess out. But once the Corvette is done properly, later applications should be kept slightly away from places where polish and wax accumulate. When you buff out, there'll be enough polish in the rag to impart gloss to the small portion skipped. This technique will work on all but the most

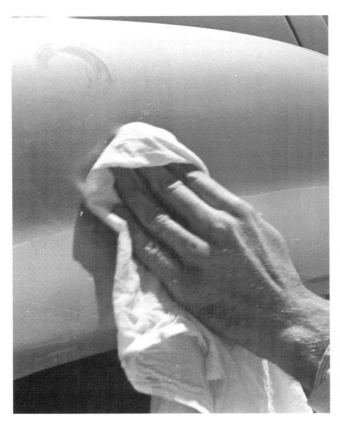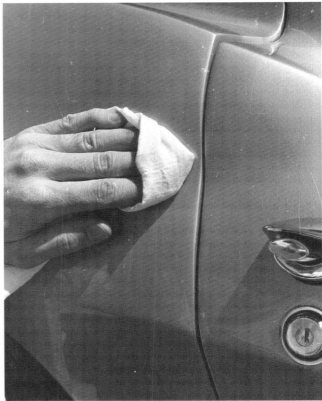

critical colors, such as black and dark metallics. Most waxes, by their very nature, will leave residue behind, though that's not true for all polishes.

A common mistake in polish and wax application is an overly generous dose. More is not better. Heavy applications leave streaks and quickly clog the applicator. Use sparingly and rub in well with moderate pressure, lightening pressure as the polish or wax begins to dry. Done properly, dried polish or wax will hardly be visible and will whisk off quickly with a clean towel.

Instructions with some polishes and waxes recommend doing small patches at a time. Others tell you to do the entire vehicle to let the product "set." I almost always do small portions. Some instructions say you must use a circular motion. Others demand back and forth. As a general rule, try back and forth to work out problem areas. Then finish up with circular. Or you could do the reverse. Combining both motions, I think, minimizes the chance the final finish will show any marks.

Proper polish and wax technique starts at the top and works down, just like washing. But if you're working outside and it appears the daylight will fade into darkness before you're done, reverse the sequence. Do the sides of the Corvette while it's still light out, leaving the top surfaces for the overhead light in your garage—or tomorrow's daylight.

Removable hardtops were introduced as Corvette options in 1956, and between 1967 and 1975 they could be ordered covered with vinyl. With vinyl, clean first like any other vinyl surface. Silicone protectants are the popular treatment for vinyl tops, but I've had good luck with Vinyl Top Wax by Turtle Wax, which looks, smells, and acts like vinyl floor wax. Be sure the vinyl top is clean, though, or the wax will protect

Above: Don't wear watches or rings when polishing or waxing. Polish or wax buildup along body seams and door edges can be avoided by keeping the polish or wax a quarter-inch or so away from edges. A clean polishing rag will hold enough residue to shine the remaining area later, providing the paint was in decent condition.

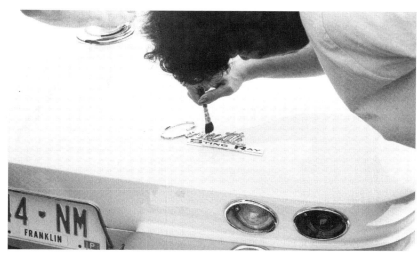

Top: *For dusting a flawless finish, nothing beats a genuine ostrich feather duster.* **Right:** *Concours detailing requires extreme attention to details. Fine brushes (often dusted with Endust) are used to remove dust and polish from scripts and emblems.*

the dirt as well as the vinyl. Painted tops should be polished and waxed just like body surfaces.

Here's another Bill Munzer tip. Bill thinks the world's best dusters are made of ostrich feathers. He uses one to dust off his Corvette just before judging. But watch out for little pieces of feather that might get lodged behind corners of chrome and emblems that could cause a points deduction.

On the subject of dusters, if you don't already have a California Duster, buy one tomorrow. Unlike Bill Munzer's final show car dusting, the California Duster is designed to be used between washings for everyday or occasional-use cars. The real McCoy uses a cotton mop-style head impregnated with paraffin wax. Steve Dangremond kept telling me to get one. I kept poo-pooing the idea. Finally he bought one for me and insisted I try it. Now I wouldn't be without it. Unless a Corvette is stored off premises, I don't cover it because I just enjoy looking at it. But uncovered, dust accumulates practically overnight, especially on dark colors. The duster grabs the dust without streaking or scratching. But I don't use it if the car has been driven in rain or on wet roads.

One last, but very easy and useful, tip. Black is my favorite color, but it and many others can be tough to polish or wax to a completely streak-free finish. Try this: Spritz the surface with water and buff again with a

If you don't already have a California Duster, buy one tomorrow.

Left: Don Williams carefully cleans polish residue from the vinyl trim strip of this midyear convertible's top stowage lid.
Above: For metal polishing, here are two favorites. Both Nevr-Dull and IBIZ Metal Polish have ingredients embedded in cloth wadding. In addition to chrome, IBIZ recommends its polish for silver, brass, pewter, stainless steel, gold, copper, aluminum, and magnesium.
Page 91 top: Shown here is more fine detailing. A camel hair brush is used to sweep dust from the ribs of a side exhaust trim panel, and a toothbrush is used to remove polish dust from the groove between a door and door trim bead.
Page 91 bottom: Sal Ricotta dabs a tiny bit of touchup paint to the taillight-surround area. Note that Sal uses his left hand to steady his right.

clean towel. That's it. I keep distilled water in a Windex bottle for this, and it really works.

Chrome and brightwork

Exterior chrome surfaces have to be exquisite on a show Corvette. If show is your goal, bumpers and bright trim may have to be removed and replated or refinished, ideally by someone specializing in auto restoration. To make good chrome sparkle, Bill Munzer cleans with PPG's Acryli-Clean, washes, then shines with Windex.

To get less-than-perfect chrome looking better, start by cleaning it along with the body surfaces. Give it the same kerosene bath, and then follow with polish. Don't use sandpaper or rubbing compound. Don't use steel wool—yet. If there are stubborn, rusty areas, try some nonabrasive household cleaner like Bon Ami or a very mild abrasive like Soft Scrub. If that doesn't do it, you might as well try steel wool. SOS will work, but a

gentler approach is 0000-grade steel wool dampened with a light oil like WD-40 (Dave Burroughs prefers G96 oil, a favorite of gun collectors). Working a rusted area the size of a quarter might reveal nothing more than a pin-sized break in the chrome. Remove the oil with a hot detergent bath. Then thoroughly dry and seal the breaks with carnauba wax. If the rust spot is larger than pin size, try dabbing a bit of high-gloss silver paint on it before waxing. This isn't a concours-winning technique, but for a

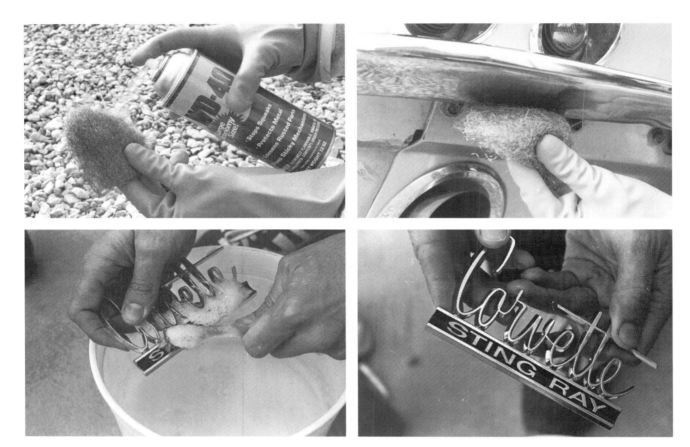

driver it will do. It also protects that area from further corrosion, improving the odds of a good plating job sometime in the future.

Glass

Techniques for cleaning exterior glass are much the same as those described earlier for interior glass, but the exterior is easier because it can be flushed with lots of water. One of the windshield debuggers made of nylon mesh and sponge works well on all glass. Dishwashing detergents have antispotting agents to help them flush clean. Once the grime is gone, use the techniques for polishing glass described in the previous chapter.

My folks grew up on farms in northern Manitoba, and they always had big barrels to catch rainwater as it came off the roof. They used the rainwater for washing things because it was soft. Did you ever notice that after washing your Corvette, the chrome and glass surfaces have to be wiped off to prevent spotting, yet after a rain shower the Corvette's glass is clean and bright? It's the water. If a Corvette is dirty and gets rained on, it will look lousy because the dirt collects in drops of the rainwater and then stays there when the drops dry. But a clean Corvette exposed to a shower often comes out looking great. If your car is stored inside, consider moving it out for a natural shower rinse and then moving it back inside for a towel dry. The glass will look beautiful. Some enthusiasts keep some captured rainwater handy for cleaning glass and chrome. If that's too much bother, or if you live in acid-rain territory, a jug of distilled water from the supermarket is inexpensive and yields the same results.

Top: Light corrosion and exhaust residue buildup on chrome can be cleaned with light oil like WD-40 and fine 0000-grit steel wool. Never use steel wool if something less abrasive will work.

Above: Corvette scripts simply must be removed periodically for proper cleaning. Start with mild detergent. If more cleaning power is needed, a mild abrasive like Soft Scrub will work wonders.

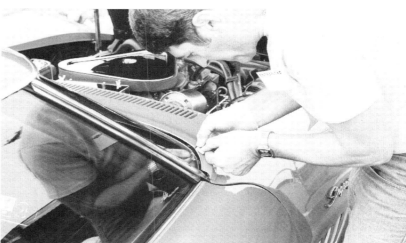

Right above: We've all seen side window glass with vertical scratches. One way these are caused is by small pieces of grit lodged in the window felt or rubber seal. Check and clean these periodically as Kathy Williams does here.

Right below: Here is Sal Ricotta again, this time delicately using a razor blade to edge the transition between painted surface and chrome bead on windshield trim.

If you can't feel the scratch with your fingernail, it can be removed.

After reading about rainwater and distilled water in this book's first edition, Tony Ricci wrote me to say that he discovered a free source of soft water. He pours the water out of his dehumidifier into plastic gallon jugs and saves it for Corvette cleaning duties.

Don't assume that a chipped or scratched windshield has to be replaced. A good glass shop has compounds for polishing scratches. I've also seen kits in the Eastwood catalog that comes packed with my *Hemmings* each month. The rule of thumb is that if you can't feel the scratch with your fingernail, it can be completely removed. If you can feel it, the opaqueness can be polished out, leaving a clean groove that's much less noticeable. A chip in glass can be repaired with something called the Novus process. It involves cleaning and polishing the cloudiness out and then filling the crack with an injection of a resin material. For a typical stone chip resembling a spider web, the resin is put in under pressure so that voids are filled. After the resin hardens, excess resin on the glass is polished. The result isn't perfect but it's quite good. It's also relatively expensive. Fixing more than two or three chips might cost nearly as much as a new windshield. But replacing a windshield often invites new problems. Stainless-steel retaining strips can get bent or scratched, and leaks are sometimes introduced. Since all auto glass is date-coded, it's nice to retain your Corvette's original glass if possible. If you do need to replace a windshield and want the correct date coding, Dale Smith's OEM Glass in Bloomington, Illinois, can oblige.

One thing that distinguishes a Corvette show car from a driver is that the glass in a show car will be clean right up to the seal. Look closely at your own Corvette right now and you're likely to see a little bit of crud on the glass right where it enters the seal. Over time, that crusty layer gets hard. To remove it, Dave Burroughs wraps a little 0000-grade steel wool around a small stick, squirts it with Windex or Dawn, and goes to work. Use this only for hard-to-reach, stubborn areas along the glass edge. For areas easier to reach, try a single-edge razor blade in a plastic holder. Both steel wool and a razor blade can damage glass, not to mention the seals, so proceed with care. John Amgwert cautions to be sure the outer seal for roll-up windows is clean. A speck of sand lodged in a door glass seal ruined the window of one of John's Corvettes.

When I wrote the first edition of this book, I hadn't personally used Rain-X, but included the comments of Milt Antonick who had and liked the product. He said that when driving in the rain, water beaded up like buckshot and blew right off the glass. Kent Brooks swears by Rain-X. He applies it to the windshield and rear glass every time he washes his car, and that's several times a week. So I've been shamed into using Rain-X and I'll tell you what I think.

First, I love the effect of driving in rain if Rain-X has been recently applied. As long as you're moving and it's not a downpour, you don't even need wipers. Like Milt said, the water just beads and blows right off. But I've given up trying to use Rain-X on windshields in summer months. It's hard enough keeping the bugs cleaned off, and Rain-X seems to compound the problem by adding to the smearing. But I use it religiously during bug-free months. The product makes no claim of preventing wiper scratching, but it seems like it would minimize the very fine abrasion marks that result from dirt being ground into the windshield by the wipers, especially when using the washers. It's important to realize that this is a glass treatment, not a cleaner. The glass must be squeaky clean before applying. And it has to be reapplied periodically to retain effectiveness.

On the downside, a reader of this book's first edition wrote me to say that after several attempts to use Rain-X on street cars, he had nothing but trouble and finally gave up. Captain L. W. Reimer said he followed the instructions to a tee, but found "that every time I try to clean the windows of my family wagon with Windex and paper towels, all I get is smeared winter grime. The glass is so slippery that the road grime just smears instead of being removed by the towel." Captain Reimer added, however, that Rain-X worked like a charm on his ship's bridge windows at sea in beading off all the salt spray and rain.

Love it or hate it, Rain-X is such an amazing product that it warrants at least trying. If you've never used it, try a small test patch on your windshield to see if it works for you and your driving patterns.

Plastics

Enthusiasts often refer to the plastic in their Corvettes as Plexiglas. It's understandable. Plexiglas is a registered product name, like Kleenex

Above: The package says it's an incredible, high-tech glass treatment. True enough. Applied to a clean windshield, it makes rain water bead up and blow off like buckshot. There's no question it makes driving in rain safer, but it probably also minimizes the light scratches that wipers eventually grind into windshields.

The glass must be squeaky clean before applying.

Above and above right: Rigid plastic like that of a Corvette's removable hardtop rear window should be washed using liberal amounts of water and light pressure. Small scratches and hazing can be removed with an auto wax containing mild abrasives.

or Scotch Tape, that has come to be used in a generic sense. To be accurate, Plexiglas is an acrylic plastic produced by Rohm and Haas Inc. Lexan is a polycarbonate plastic produced by General Electric. Different plastics have different characteristics. We'll generalize here and call them either flexible, like that in some Corvette convertible rear windows, or rigid, like that in a taillight lens or a Corvette's removable hardtop's rear window. Keep in mind that rigid plastic isn't necessarily very hard.

Never use a metallic object on plastic. Don't even use a nylon-covered bug sponge. Plastics are much softer than glass. Their softness permits scratches to be removed and new ones to be put in. The optional, transparent roof panels of 1984 and newer Corvettes are rigid plastic and deserve the same kind of care. Optional glass T-tops for 1978–1982 Corvettes are genuine glass, but some aftermarket tops are plastic, too.

The correct way to wash plastic is to drench it thoroughly with water before putting a washcloth or sponge against it. Use minimal pressure, and let the dirt float away with lots of water. Use a dabbing motion, not a back-and-forth rub.

Both rigid types of plastic found in a Corvette's removable hardtop and the flexible type found in convertible top windows are prone to scratching and dulling with age, but both can be renewed. If damage is

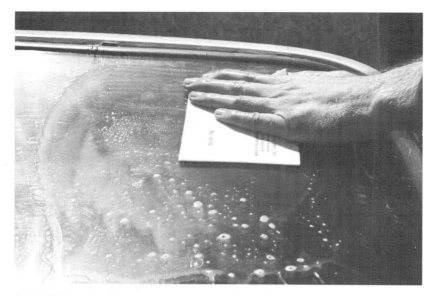

Left: *When scratches can't be removed with conventional polish or wax, something more abrasive must be used. Here is a demonstration using a series of Polysand's abrasive pads to remove a deep scratch. The trick is to get to the depth of the scratch, then use progressively finer abrasives to remove the scratches newly introduced. Keep in mind that if the scratches are very deep, they can be removed, but some distortion might result.*

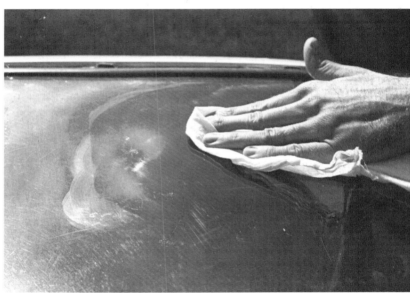

Right: The finest Polysand abrasive pad leaves a surface that is almost clear. Finishing up with polish restores the plastic surface to like-new.

Heat can stretch or distort plastic materials.

slight, you may get by with your favorite polish or wax. John Amgwert says nothing beats Meguiar's Sealer and Reseal Glaze for polishing Plexiglas and plastic. Dave Burroughs says the same about Ultra Finish. Personally, I'd start with my favorite overall wax, IBIZ. All of these products will remove fine scratches and leave a clear, shiny, and protected finish. But if the scratches are deeper, you'll need to invest more time to get them out. They can be removed as long as they're not too deep.

Removing scratches from plastic is a matter of abrading the surface around the scratch down to the bottom of the scratch, and then removing any new scratches introduced by continuing to work the area with a graduated series of finer abrasives. The final abrasive is a fine polish, such as jeweler's rouge. Rubbing compound and a power buffer will work on some plastics, but it's tricky. Power buffing creates heat, and heat can scorch and stretch plastic materials.

For those who like having all the right tools for the job, I can tell you of two different kits of materials designed specifically for removing scratches

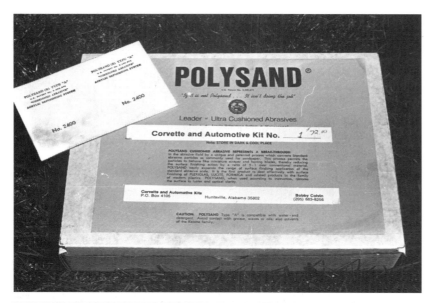

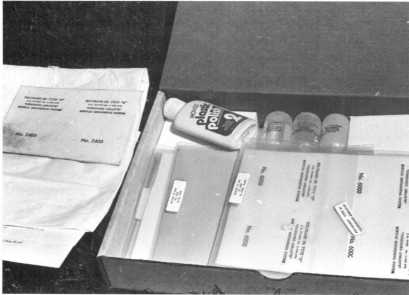

from plastic. One is Polysand, developed by Corvette enthusiast Bobby Colvin's company, Corvette and Automotive Kits. The other is Micro-mesh, sold in plastics stores around the country. Polysand contains spongy-backed abrasive pads of several grits and several bottles of polishing and stain-removing fluids. Micro-mesh contains several grades of abrasive sheets, a foam pad, and polishing fluid. These kits and many other plastic polishing materials are also available from mailorder aircraft supply companies such as Aircraft Spruce & Specialty Company.

Do some experimenting and use the finest abrasive that will do the job. On flexible plastic, use light pressure to avoid stretching. This is especially important if you're working on a warm day. On cold days, flexible plastic gets stiff and can crack. Remember this possibility of cracking when using a convertible top on very cold days.

All of the techniques mentioned for plastic windows work for other plastic parts, like taillight lenses and plastic trim, provided the color is all

Above left: Polysand is a kit containing spongy-backed abrasive pads of several grits and several bottles of polishing and stain-removing liquids for plastic.
Above center: Micromesh is another plastic restoration kit, less expensive and less complete than Polysand, but also very good. It has several grades of abrasive sheets, a foam backing pad, and polishing fluid.
Above top: Novus #3 is a heavy scratch remover; #2 is a fine scratch remover; #1 cleans and shines, and contains antifog, antistatic, and dust repellent ingredients.
Above lower: Aircraft Spruce specializes in aircraft products. Because plexiglass cleaning and restoration is such a major part of aircraft maintenance, Aircraft Spruce's catalog includes numerous plastic polishes and refurbishing kits, including all three of the products mentioned above.

Above: *Sid Savage is an auto dealer supply company. Most items it sells are of little use to an individual Corvette owner, but Sid Savage White Wall & Vinyl Concentrate is a great cleaner for tires of any marque.*
Right: *Stoner is best known for its tire dressing, Stoner More Shine Less Time For Tires. But it also sells this detailing kit with specialized cleaners. The kit includes silicone and non-silicone vinyl, plastic and rubber cleaners, carpet cleaner, glass cleaner, trim cleaner, and tar, grease, and sap cleaner.*

the way through. These parts can be removed for buffing on a wheel. Use a light touch because buffing wheels can burn plastic.

Tires

Tires often show the difference between a Corvette that's been cleaned and one that's been detailed, whether for show, street, or resale. Some owners ignore tires because they're not really part of the car. Right? Concours people know better. They know that spotless tires are a must for a successful presentation. When a potential buyer sees tires on a Corvette for sale that look ready for concours judging, the buyer will instinctively figure a car-care fanatic has owned the car and everything must be in tip-top shape. I'm not talking about that awful tire paint slopped on by used-car dealers in the old days. I'm talking about spotlessly clean rubber with just the right amount of sheen. Tires should complement wheels and body surfaces, not detract from or overpower them.

Here is Dave Burroughs' old procedure for making anything from street rubber to off-the-shelf new tires look fantastic. Start with a scrub brush, a bucket of hot water, Dawn dishwashing detergent, and a hose. Rinse the tire. Then squirt pure Dawn directly onto it. Brush it in well. Then hose down and repeat until the grime is gone. A whitewall or white letter, redline, or goldline won't look perfect yet. A blackwall might, but continue with the following steps regardless. Wipe excess water off the tires (but not the wheels). Then squirt on a good whitewall bleaching cleaner. Dave uses one called Sid Savage White Wall & Vinyl Concentrate mixed fifty-fifty with water. Westley's Bleche Wite is my choice. Brush using a tight, circular motion. Do the entire tire, right out to the tread.

Don't let the tire bleach soak too long. Tire-bleaching products contain warnings about damage to aluminum and magnesium wheels and painted surfaces. I've never had a problem with either, but I keep the wheels and adjacent body surfaces wet and I rinse everything off quickly and thoroughly.

Now dry the tires and saturate with silicone protectant full strength. Let it soak in for at least a half an hour—all day wouldn't hurt. If it doesn't stay wet, apply more. Finish the job by rinsing off the excess silicone and polishing the tire with a dry towel. This technique gives tires the semigloss, natural look for show, street, or resale.

As I mentioned, that was Dave's old technique. Since he's gotten back into aircraft restoration, he uses Spartan BH38 Cleaner/Degreaser for almost all automotive cleaning tasks, including tires.

You'll be able to maintain tires treated this way for quite a while by just washing with a mild cleaner. In fact, after Dave Burroughs has a Corvette the way he wants it, he just uses clear water in the evening with no soap whatever for the entire exterior, including the tires.

Here's my shortcut for good-looking tires. After washing your Corvette's exterior, give the tires a scrub with a tire bleach like Westley's or Sid's. Dry the tires and then spray with Stoner More Shine Less Time For Tires. This is the best spray-and-walk-away tire product I've ever used.

It is quick and effective with just the right sheen.

100

Pages 100 and 101: The Corvette wheel and tire shown have been removed to stage these photos, but removal is certainly an excellent way to thoroughly clean a tire now and then. The first step is to soak the rubber with a tire cleaner—Westley's Bleche-Wite is used here. The name may imply that this is exclusively for whitewalls, but it works beautifully for blackwalls too. A scrub brush combined with Bleche-Wite is all that's needed for most tires. SOS might be necessary for curb scuffs. Keep wheels wet to avoid spotting, and thoroughly rinse. Dry the tire and wheel with towels, then apply silicone as described in the text.

For a daily Corvette driver, this is a little pricey, but quick and effective with just the right sheen.

One of the old-timer tricks for making tires look good was brake fluid. It does work, but brake fluid is murder on paint. With all the excellent other choices available today, there's no reason to risk it. Ditto for lacquer thinner.

Should you pick all the little pebbles from the tire treads for concours showing? To play it safe, yes. Most shows will deduct for stones in tire treads. At Bloomington or an NCRS event, a few won't matter. These judging formats follow the "factory-original" concept. At the St. Louis assembly plant, at least, Corvettes were driven outside on the way to the water-test booth (where most leaked, by the way). So really astute judges

Left: A quick spray of a silicone tire dressing is fine for a street car. For show though, hand application of silicone treatment is better, and serious contenders use Q-tips and soft cloths to smooth the silicone into each groove, front and back.

know it was possible for a few stones to have lodged in the tire treads during that brief passage through factory-original status. Sounds reasonable to me.

Steel wheels and hubcaps

Wheels are something else that have to look good for overall show-car effect. For steel wheels and hubcaps, clean the hubcaps as you would any other exterior brightwork. A few high-performance suspension packages for early Corvettes had small hubcaps with a lot of wheel showing, but it usually is just the small lip between the wheelcover and tire. Even so, the exposed wheel portion should look good. The best way to renew a badly scraped wheel is to remove the tire from the wheel and strip the wheel to bare metal using paint stripper. Reprime and repaint the wheel in its original color.

Protect the rim from scuffing when the tire is reinstalled by covering it with easily removable tape. Any decent tire store today has the type of

Right: *Latex glove, soft rag, aerosol glass cleaner—the way to properly clean a Corvette's wire wheelcover.*

Don't expect the tape to stick if the tire has been treated with silicone.

installation machines made for mag or chrome wheels which pull the tire onto the wheel without touching the wheel rim lip. You can have this done for standard steel wheels that you've refinished.

The shortcut technique is to paint the wheel with the tire mounted. The difficult part is masking the tire effectively. A decent job can be done by relieving masking tape every quarter inch with small cuts so it will conform to the rim curvature. Don't expect the tape to stick if the tire has been treated with silicone.

The contributors offer some other wheel-painting ideas. Bill Munzer says if you don't want to break the tire bead, use 1/4-inch masking tape to mask the tire and poke the tape behind the rim edge with something pointed. Then use 3/4-inch masking tape over the quarter-inch. Tuck newspaper under the outside edge of the wider masking tape. Bill further suggests removing the tape as soon as the paint is tacky so it doesn't soak through the tape onto the tire. John Amgwert suggests breaking the tire

Left and above: Keeping Corvette alloy wheels looking great is a lot easier with the right wheel cleaners. Eagle One's wheel cleaners are among the best, but be sure to select the right one for your needs. The A2Z Wheel Cleaner shown—uniform wheel care symbol C—has a formula safe for all wheels and is the correct choice for Corvette wheels with clear coats.

bead but leaving the tire on and coating the tire with thin grease before painting the wheel. No masking tape is required as the paint won't stick to the greased tire. Be careful not to slop any grease on the rim, because the paint won't stick there either. Milt Antonick used to make a mask of aluminum foil for wheels, but now he prefers to remove the tire, refinish the wheel, and then have the tire store use the mag-wheel machine to reinstall the tire without scratching the wheel. More costly, but the results are the best.

Knock-off, bolt-on, and other cast wheels

If you own a midyear Corvette with an original set of knock-off or bolt-on wheels, your wheels are worth more than some of your neighbors' cars. Aluminum wheels in excellent condition should be cleaned with a mild detergent solution. For a thorough cleaning, Dave Burroughs scrubs his wheels in the bathtub and uses a handheld, flexible showerhead for a hot rinse. Dave has found that the original paint on 1965–1967 Corvette aluminum wheels can be freshened by soaking in Armor All. Provided scratches or dings aren't deep, the fin edges and rim sections can be wet-sanded with 600-grit sandpaper, using WD-40 or G-96 as the lubricant. Follow the 600-grit with steel wool (or start with the steel wool for minor scratches). Then finish with Semichrome or Mother's Mag & Aluminum Polish. Observe the machining marks in the wheel's bright surfaces, and

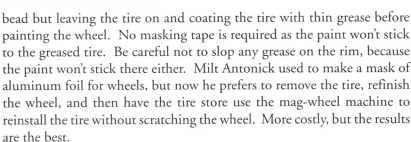

Your wheels are worth more than your neighbor's car.

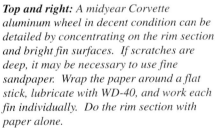

Top and right: A midyear Corvette aluminum wheel in decent condition can be detailed by concentrating on the rim section and bright fin surfaces. If scratches are deep, it may be necessary to use fine sandpaper. Wrap the paper around a flat stick, lubricate with WD-40, and work each fin individually. Do the rim section with paper alone.

Above: After wheels are freshened, Eagle One Etching Mag Cleaner—uniform wheel care symbol B— will keep them looking beautiful. This product is designed for wheels without a clear coating, and this applies to midyear knock-off and bolt-on aluminum wheels. If your midyear aluminum wheels are concours quality and are not exposed to street use, Eagle One's A2Z cleaner described on page 104 is milder and will work fine.

follow the same direction when sanding and polishing for a natural factory appearance.

Wheels with more damage will require more extensive reworking. David Cosner, a Corvette enthusiast who specializes in restoring 1963–1967 Corvette aluminum wheels, has perfected a technique he's happy to share with others. He can also restore your wheels, or you can buy wheels he's already restored. Cosner puts a minimum of twenty-five hours of hand labor into each wheel, and his work is magnificent. Briefly, here's how he does it.

Start by removing all dings. Small ones can be filed out. Deeper ones must have metal added by the heliarc process. For knock-off wheels, the knock-off spinner may need metal filling before replating as well. Glass-bead the wheels. If they're 1965–1967 wheels with paint, make sure every bit of old paint is removed. You can also chemically strip the paint, but

Left: *Follow the sandpaper with steel wool and a metal polish such as Simichrome, Nevr-Dull, Mother's Mag & Aluminum Polish, or IBIZ. By the way, Dave Burroughs thinks steel wool shouldn't be used on non-coated alloy wheels because he thinks it is bad to mix metals. He prefers synthetic steel wool pads made by 3M.*

it's more difficult. Do not sandblast. Clean the outer rim surface and the leading edges of all fins with a flat file. Use a progression of 220-grit to 600-grit wet-dry sandpaper to sand the outer rim lip and leading edges of all fins. Use the paper dry. Start at the valve stem hole and go all around the wheel very thoroughly. After the sandpaper, use Simichrome to polish to a high sheen. The surfaces should be perfect. They'll polish to look like chrome. Wash the wheel thoroughly to get rid of all the dirt and polish. The Semichrome tends to stick in corners. Get all of it out. Let the wheels dry completely.

If it's a 1965–1967 wheel, it has to be painted. Use a finger to coat the surfaces not to be painted with WD-40, applying it very carefully. You must not let the WD-40 run onto surfaces to be painted because the paint won't stick. For 1967 bolt-ons, cut a plastic or cardboard form and place it on the center of the wheel where the cover attaches to catch overspray; that part of the wheel shouldn't be painted. The proper paint for 1965–1967 Corvette aluminum wheels has a very high metallic content. It tends to clog nozzles, and that's why, according to Dave Cosner, the spray bombs usually don't spray on enough of a metallic look. Dave buys

The proper paint for 1965–1967 aluminum wheels has a high metallic content.

Right: The finish achieved with polish and steel wool closely matches the original factory look which did show light machining marks. If polishing is continued using soft rags, the finish will eventually look like chrome. This is a classic case of "what the factory should have done." It didn't, but highly polished midyear aluminum wheels are spectacular.

Pick the paint off with a fingernail.

the paint in bulk and sprays it with a commercial gun and compressor, but still fights clogging and spitting.

Put plenty of paint on, but avoid runs. Spray with the wheel in a vertical position, not flat. If the wheel is vertical and the gun spits, the heavy paint glob might fall short of the wheel. If you spray into the wheel flat, the globs *will* fall into the wheel. The hardest area to coat is the inner peripheral surface. Dave sprays that while rolling the wheel.

As soon as the wheel is painted, start removing the paint from the surfaces coated with WD-40. Don't try to use lacquer thinner or abrasives. Remember, these surfaces were highly polished and they've been coated with a light dose of WD-40. Pick the paint off with a fingernail. For the fins, pick toward the center of the fin so the paint won't peel down into the surface that's supposed to stay painted.

The special machines that pull tires onto mag wheels without touching the outer rim surface are ideal for remounting Corvette bolt-on or knock-off wheels after they've been redone. Some Corvette purists hand-mount their aluminum wheels. Be most wary of conventional mounting-demounting machines like those still found in some gas stations. These

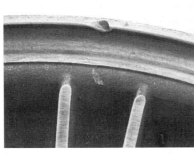

Left: Full restoration of wheels requires that all dings be removed. Small ones can be sanded out. Larger ones, like those at far left, must have metal added by the heliarc process (near left). After the weld is filed and sanded, the repair will be invisible.
Below: *For reference, shown is a new-old-stock (NOS) bolt-on Corvette aluminum wheel which has been safely stored since 1967. Notice the very high metallic content of the paint and the visible machining on the rim section.*

This repair is beyond do-it-yourself.

have a gripper that can easily snap a chunk off the rim section of a Corvette's aluminum wheel when demounting. When mounting, a slide bar scrapes the outer rim edge unless it's protected by tape (and sometimes even then). Some tire stores deal with this by slipping a protective plastic sheath over the bar. I could maybe live with that for a steel wheel, but not a cast alloy.

With the exception of the 1982 Collector Edition's special wheel that resembled 1967's bolt-on, aluminum wheels for other Corvettes have had more conventional designs, usually a machined surface with a clear coat. If this style wheel is bent, specialty shops can straighten it. For more severe damage, these wheels can be straightened and completely refinished. To do it properly, the wheel has to be repaired, machined, cleared, and baked. This is beyond do-it-yourself. There are often ads for wheel specialty shops in publications like *AutoWeek*. I shipped two wheels to Ye Ole Wheel Shop with good results, before realizing a local independent shop was equally good. Be advised that fixing a slight out-of-round condition is not too expensive, but complete wheel refinishes are.

Convertible tops

Convertible tops deteriorate because they're seldom cared for properly. Nothing is worse for a soft top than to fold it down while it's damp or dirty. The window gets scarred and the canvas gets scrunched against itself with abrasive dirt between the folds. Life is short and convertibles should be enjoyed, but if you're finicky like me and want your original top to last, start making it standard practice to never fold a convertible top unless it's clean and dry. If yours is a Corvette convertible with a removable hardtop for winter use, take the convertible top out completely and store it in an unfolded position when the hardtop is in use. Mark the position of the convertible top's mounting brackets before removing. John Amgwert thinks it's a good idea to spray the *inside* of convertible tops with Scotchguard.

Products are available for cleaning convertible tops, and they work fine. For persistent stains try some of the products made for cleaning plastic bathroom showers and tubs, like Soft Scrub or Dow Bathroom Cleaner with "scrubbing bubbles." These have good stain-removing qualities without harsh abrasives. Soft Scrub has a mild abrasive. Dow's product has no abrasive but does have some bleach, so be careful around the rear window. Dave Burroughs says his old standby, Sid Savage's Auto Cleaner, is great for convertible tops.

Here's one more exterior detailing tip from Don Williams for convertible tops. Don keeps a black permanent-ink marker in his show-car detailing kit. If the piping on a black convertible top cracks slightly, revealing white threading, a dab of the marker will hide it. The same holds for tiny nicks on black chassis parts or black window moldings. Don't go overboard with this. Marker ink looks slightly blue against pure black. This is strictly for minor touch-up.

Above: Felt tip markers can be used for touchups, but only small ones. Buy these from an art supply store, not from a supermarket; an art supplier will have a much better selection. This one, made by Berol, is double-ended. Be sure the ink is permanent.

Chapter 5

Follow-up

A healthy dose of elbow grease and know-how has your Corvette looking great. With this time and effort invested, it makes sense to maintain your Corvette in pristine condition. Keeping it there isn't too difficult, but nothing will preserve your Corvette in the condition it was when new or just freshly refurbished. Its condition deteriorates constantly.

A Corvette is a little like the human body, but the analogy is far from perfect. For one thing, a Corvette starts to deteriorate from the day it's built, whereas our bodies start downhill sometime after maturity. And although the process is essentially irreversible for us, a Corvette can be brought back to better than new. Then the deterioration cycle starts all over.

Proper care can appreciably extend the quality and length of life for our bodies and Corvettes. Care includes the right fuel, proper protection from the elements, and the right amount and type of exercise. Of course, nothing is guaranteed, either for us or for our cars. You can take excellent care of your body and still check out twenty years before your couch-potato, beer-guzzling neighbor. But taking care of yourself definitely swings the odds in your favor.

With Corvettes, a number of things can be done to slow deterioration. However, there is no assurance that even with the proper care deterioration won't be excessive. Besides, there is always disagreement over what constitutes *proper* care.

What one thing keeps a Corvette in the best possible condition? Being driven. A twenty-year-old Corvette with 5 miles on the odometer makes an interesting story. But the same Corvette with 20,000 miles accumulated in weekly 20-mile trips would be in much better condition. Things can be done to help preserve a Corvette subjected to extended storage—we'll get to them in a moment—but nothing beats regular exercise. Starting a Corvette's engine now and then helps, but it isn't enough. The engine

Nothing beats regular exercise.

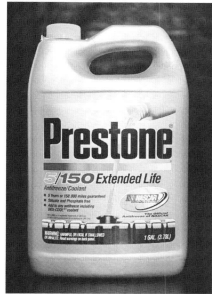

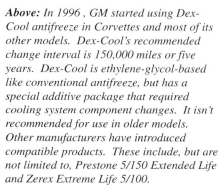

Above: In 1996 , GM started using Dex-Cool antifreeze in Corvettes and most of its other models. Dex-Cool's recommended change interval is 150,000 miles or five years. Dex-Cool is ethylene-glycol-based like conventional antifreeze, but has a special additive package that required cooling system component changes. It isn't recommended for use in older models. Other manufacturers have introduced compatible products. These include, but are not limited to, Prestone 5/150 Extended Life and Zerex Extreme Life 5/100.

and driveline need to be brought up to operating temperature and kept there for a while. Ten miles is adequate, and some of it should be at highway speed. If the Corvette has air conditioning, it should be turned on. All a/c systems have small amounts of lubricant suspended in their refrigerant and need to be operated at regular intervals to maintain effectiveness. You should also run the heater a while to circulate coolant through the heater core.

Storage and maintenance

If a Corvette must be stored for more than a few months, first perform all routine maintenance. This includes lubricating the chassis, changing oil and filter, and checking all fluid levels. A 1967 coupe I owned for fifteen years saw only about 400 miles annually, but I always did the things just mentioned. Plus, I flushed the cooling system and replaced the antifreeze every autumn and spring. Overkill? Probably, but the cost is minimal, especially if you do the work yourself. Have you checked the cost of a replacement 1967 radiator lately?

In 1996, GM switched the coolant in most of its cars including Corvettes to Dex-Cool, which GM developed jointly with Texaco. In the C5 Corvette, the suggested change interval for Dex-Cool was a staggering 150,000 miles or five years. Dex-Cool is ethylene-glycol-based like conventional antifreeze, but uses a special additive package without silicates. Its color is a distinctive orange-red. GM specifies that Dex-Cool shouldn't be mixed with conventional antifreeze. As for use in other years, GM states that it is okay for use in 1994 and 1995 models (except Saturn, Geo and 4-cylinder Cavaliers), but that it must be changed every two years or 30,000 miles. GM does not recommend it at all for pre-1994 models. Why those restrictions? Because cooling system modifications were necessary to accommodate the additive package in Dex-Cool. Use in earlier models could damage the cooling system.

Other antifreeze manufacturers have introduced formulas compatible with Dex-Cool. These are also an orange-red color. The labels on these products are a little vague as to use in older cars, but a call to their toll-free assistance lines or a check of their web sites will reveal cautions about using these long-life antifreezes in some cars. Talking with antifreeze experts will generally result in two pieces of advice: First, never mix antifreeze colors. The color designates the additive package family regardless of manufacturer. Second, use the antifreeze type recommended for your vehicle. Sounds obvious, but the danger is thinking that expensive, long-life formulas would be better for an older model. Not so.

There is honest disagreement about the proper tack to take with fuel for long-term storage. Some people believe the tank should be topped to prevent moisture from accumulating in the empty portion; others prefer to leave the tank dry or with just a few gallons in it. The fear of corrosion points me toward leaving the tank full, but this isn't without problems.

The first danger is that the fuel will somehow leak out. Vapors from gasoline are extremely volatile. If there's a furnace or hot water heater with a live flame in the vicinity, one colossal explosion could result. It nearly happened in a building where I rented an office-warehouse. Another tenant, who specialized in four-wheel-drive repair, pulled a Blazer into his work area one night after an off-road event, not realizing he'd punched a small hole in the fuel tank. Early the next morning, an employee walked up to the building, cigarette in hand, but the fumes were so strong he sensed the problem before opening the door.

The second problem with fuel storage is that gasoline eventually turns to a gel and can leave a varnish accumulation throughout the entire system. This isn't the end of the world, but the whole fuel system, including the tank, may have to be removed for cleaning. Additives such as Sta-bil, Fuel Fresh, and Panef Gas Stabilizer are designed to prevent gas from going bad. Aviation fuel doesn't go bad, nor does "white" gas. The problem with the latter two is locating them in your area. Despite the effort, some action should be taken to prevent sour gas from fouling a Corvette's fuel system if long-term storage is in the cards.

Is storage over the winter considered long term? For fuel concerns, I don't think so. Gas won't go bad over a few months unless it was old when purchased. But this does remind me of a couple of tips passed on to me by an old salt during my service-station employment days. He told me never to gas up at a station when the tanker was filling the underground tanks because debris that normally settles to the bottom of the tank will be stirred up. He also advised buying from the newest station in town because its tanks would be the cleanest. The latter point should be moot now. In 1988, the Federal EPA gave all stations nationwide ten years to change or modify underground tanks so that new corrosion and leakage standards would be met. But in checking with my state's enforcement agency, I have been told that a substantial percentage of service station owners have not complied. So maybe the old salt's advice still stands.

You've heard the expression "stored on blocks." Should you do it? It depends on the length of storage time. If storage is just for the winter, leaving the Corvette on its tires will enable it to be started easily and moved around, even if just in the garage area. That's not as good as an outside drive, but allowing the engine to come up to temperature, even if it's just with the rear end poking out the back of the garage, beats cold

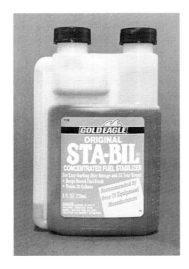

Above: One problem with long storage is that pump gasoline can eventually go "sour" and turn to a gel. Draining fuel systems avoids this, but increases the possibility of rust. Additives such as Sta-bil are designed to prevent fuel from going bad.

Above: Dave Burroughs likes to put Marvel Mystery Oil into spark plug holes as a cylinder lubricant prior to Corvette storage. **Right:** Before long storage, leave Pledge-soaked cleaning rags and a lemon air freshener inside. Don't leave them in there for the duration of storage. Just a week or so prior to storing is adequate.

storage. If storage is for a longer period, putting a Corvette on blocks is a good idea.

The term "blocks" refers to concrete blocks that can be used. I keep an extra set of jack stands around for this, but put a short section of two-by-four lumber between the stand and frame to avoid dents or scratches. The intent of the elevation is not just to take weight off the tires, but to take weight off the suspension, especially the bearings and springs. The Corvette need not be completely suspended off the ground. Six inches of chassis lift is adequate.

Speaking of tires, old-car museums inflate them with nitrogen gas to reduce oxidation. That's a trifle exotic for me, but it apparently helps. If your Corvette is a relic with the original skins, check it out.

What's not optional for long-term storage is the need to coat the interior cylinder walls with oil. There are two ways to do this, and the safe bet is to do both. The first is to stall the Corvette out by pouring oil in a slowly increasing volume into the carburetor. Observe which throats are delivering fuel at idle and pour the oil in there. You can use lightweight motor oil. The late Sam Folz of the National Corvette Restorers Society recommended a fifty-fifty mix of kerosene and Casite. Dave Burroughs likes Marvel Mystery Oil. The second and better way (and the only way for fuel injection) to get lubricant into the cylinder walls is the direct approach. Remove the spark plugs and squirt a few ounces of oil directly into the spark plug holes. Bump the starter to distribute the oil. Then replace the plugs. I'm told there are special devices that can be inserted into the plug holes (in place of the plugs) during storage that help absorb

Left: Restoration Battery Company sells batteries that have the correct construction, appearance, and date codes for virtually all vintage Corvette models. The company is represented at major Corvette shows.

any moisture present in the cylinder chamber areas, but I've not tried them. To use both techniques to coat cylinder walls, start with the carb-stalling routine and then follow with oil into the plug holes.

Batteries tend to be a problem when a Corvette is stored, and a lot of people advise removing the battery completely. I usually don't. Let's understand the issues involved. Batteries discharge on their own. Data sheets from Restoration Battery Company state that at room temperature a battery will lose about half its charge in two-and-a-half months. But at colder temperatures, the discharge rate slows dramatically. A half-charged battery will freeze at –10°F, but fully charged it can withstand –75°F. So even if the Corvette is in cold storage, the battery can stay in the car provided the charge is maintained. This appeals to me because some Corvette batteries are such a pain to remove.

In older Corvettes, about the only battery drain from the car is the clock. But an old car is an old car, and sometimes a mystery gremlin drains off some additional juice. The solution is to install a battery-disconnect switch. Even though they were never original equipment, the NCRS will not deduct points for them because they make so much sense for the storage schedules of so many older Corvettes. They save post connectors from wearing out from repeated use, and they eliminate sparking at the post connections. The engine diagnostics and other electronics of newer Corvettes really argue for not disconnecting or removing the battery at all. You can, but a better solution is a charger with an automatic circuit that shuts down when the battery is fully charged

A half-charged battery will freeze at -10°F, but a fully charged battery can withstand -75°F.

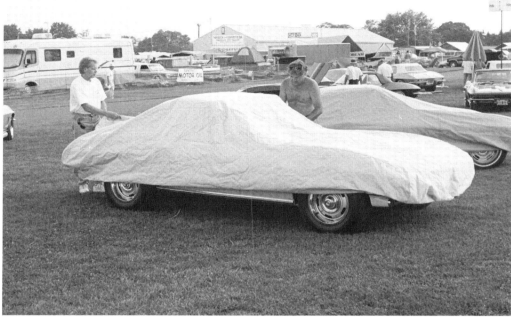

Top: *D-con helps insure that mice won't eat interiors and engine compartment wiring during storage.*
Above: *De-Moist is a hardware store product designed to keep closets dry, but it works fine for Corvette interiors during storage.*
Right: *Car covers are most often associated with storage, but these concours entrants are using a cover to keep a pristine Corvette free of dust.*

and comes back on when needed. As long as you have an electrical source in your storage area, this can be left on the battery all the time. Tom Tucker's 1987 Corvette, which he's had since new, averages only about 500 miles per year but was going through numerous batteries, apparently because they'd completely discharge between visits. Tom now leaves an automatic charger on the battery during storage and battery life is normal.

Another bit of wisdom from old-timers hanging around the station where I worked was that storing a battery on concrete would suck the juice right out of it. According to Restoration Battery, this is true for old-style batteries with rubber cases, but not for newer batteries with plastic cases. Restoration Battery says storing on a cool concrete floor is actually a good idea, but suggests an insulating piece of plywood for rubber cases.

The housewares department of the local hardware store carries products designed to keep closets dry, and they work great in the interiors of stored Corvettes. One I use is called De-Moist. It's a 12-ounce cloth bag of moisture absorber which can be reused indefinitely by baking it in an oven to drive out moisture. I've seen other kits that consist of little perforated metal cans into which absorbent material is added and changed when necessary.

I don't like the smell of mothballs, but some people use them. An open box of baking soda is a safe way to minimize odors without introducing any new ones. You can also use an air freshener, but don't leave it in there indefinitely. A week is sufficient.

John Amgwert puts a box of d-con mice killer in the engine compartment and interior of each car he stores. John has seen interiors ruined by mice, and mice built a nest in the air cleaner of one of his own Corvettes. I should have listened to him. Mice swiped some pink fiberglass insulation from somewhere and then built a nest under the fuel injection tunnels of my 1985 Corvette a few years back. No damage, but there were some strange odors for a while. John suggests checking a stored Corvette occasionally for mouse droppings; if you find any, you've got a

problem. If you use d-con, start looking for dead mice. If none are apparent, look for evidence of nest activity.

Radiators are another source of honest debate about storing full or empty. I prefer to flush before and after storage, and I keep the radiator topped with antifreeze at all times. But some enthusiasts prefer to store with the cooling system drained. Jim Paxton got tired of the mess every time he drained his midyear Corvette's radiator, so he rigged up a conventional household spigot to the lower radiator hose. Now, he can hook up a hose and drain the radiator without spilling a drop on the Corvette's undercarriage or his garage floor. Best you not try to convince a concours judge that this was a rare factory option, however.

When storing a convertible Corvette with its soft top, leave the top up if possible. The windows of a stored Corvette, convertible or otherwise, should be left up, but with an inch opening at the top. Generally, a Corvette should be covered with something that breathes. A fitted cover is fine, as are old cotton sheets. Another option, though, is to seal the Corvette in an airtight bag. With this setup, you drive the Corvette into the opened bag, toss in a couple of moisture absorbers, then seal the whole works. Milt Antonick has tried this for a car he stores in a lousy garage with a dirt floor, and says it works great. The specific product he uses is Omnibag, sold by Pine Ridge Enterprises. The company also sells CarJacket, a premium storage bag that closes with a zipper, and MotoJacket for motorcycles. John Schoepke, Pine Ridge's owner, says he came up with these products because he constantly fought moisture problems with his own cars that were stored in farm buildings at his place in Michigan. So

Above: John Schoepke lives on a farm in Michigan and fought moisture problems for years when he stored his collector cars in barns and outbuildings. So he developed a moistureproof bag for completely sealing a stored car. His company is Pine Ridge Enterprises. The product shown is CarJacket, a premium storage bag that zips closed. The company sells a less expensive car storage bag called Omnibag, and also MotoJacket for motorcycles.

Above: A quality stainless steel exhaust system will last almost forever, and speciality companies can fashion stainless systems for virtually any Corvette model. Major Corvette shows are always well represented by muffler manufacturers and buying at a show permits a close inspection of all parts before purchase.

Have a fire extinguisher handy.

here's yet another ingenious product developed by an auto enthusiast with a need.

If your stored car isn't covered, try to limit its exposure to direct sunlight. The ideal storage area is humidity-controlled, as high moisture in the air creates nice mold-growing conditions and increases the chance of surface rust. Tires should be covered.

When a Corvette is stored but started occasionally, a new exhaust system can rot out in short order from condensation. Bill Munzer minimizes this problem by drilling a small drain hole in the lowest part of his Corvette's mufflers. For most Corvettes, this will be at the lower end of the muffler's back plate. I'm of the opinion that drilling a muffler might start corrosion at that point, so I wouldn't do it. Newer Corvettes have a lot of stainless steel in their exhaust systems, so corrosion is much less of a problem. The Corvette aftermarket has complete stainless-steel systems for virtually all Corvette models, and the quality ones will literally last forever.

Restarting a Corvette after storage isn't always easy. First, look under the car to see if there are any signs of fluid leaks. Remove the plugs and squirt oil into the cylinders again. Let it soak a while (overnight wouldn't hurt). Then spin the engine with the starter. If you've detailed your engine, put the plugs back in when turning the engine over or oil will spit out the plug holes. If you don't care, the engine will spin easier with the plugs out. When ready to start, make sure the plugs are clean and the crankcase oil is at the proper level. Start the engine. Cliff Gottlob, with thirty years of racing experience, recommends bringing the engine up to 2000 rpm immediately to get oil to the upper surfaces quickly. My thinking is old school, so I'd just let it idle for a while. But most everyone agrees that the engine shouldn't be taken to high rpm when first started. If it sounds okay, let it come up to normal operating temperature. Then shut it off and change the oil. The quick-start products you spray into the carburetor do work, but some people think they're bad for the engine. They are, for certain, extremely flammable, and that trait alone is enough for me to keep them away from a Corvette. A little fuel dribbled directly into the carburetor for priming is okay, but be sure to replace the air cleaner before starting. Have a fire extinguisher handy.

Fuel

There's no question that what comes out of automobile tailpipes is hazardous to our health. Ironically, one of the worst fuel additives with respect to health was one of the best in terms of what it did for the performance and longevity of an automobile's engine. Starting in the 1920s, the addition of tetraethyl lead to gasoline by refiners was an inexpensive way to boost octane. Moreover, the lead provided a lubricating cushion between an engine's exhaust valves and seats to minimize seat wear. The EPA mandated the reduction of tetraethyl lead in fuel starting in the early seventies, and as of January 1, 1996, it is now unavailable for automotive use in all fifty states. This is good news for our health, not so good for our pre-1971 Corvettes. But there are remedies.

The two areas of concern are octane and valve seat protection. Other than adding real tetraethyl lead yourself in the form of an additive (it's

getting awfully difficult to find), dealing with lead's removal will involve more than one approach. Let's tackle octane first. So long as leaded fuel was available, even with sharply reduced lead content, mixing three parts unleaded premium with one part leaded would yield a fuel with greater octane than either of the two fuels individually. Don't ask why, but it's a fact, and Shell Oil Company published data to prove it. This was good enough for many easily driven Corvettes while leaded pump fuel was still available. In most areas of the country, you can buy premiun unleaded pump fuel with reasonably high octane. This is adequate for many older Corvettes, particularly if timing is retarded slightly. But if it's not, two viable alternatives remain. The first is use of an octane-boosting additive. An additive such as Moroso's Octane Booster will add two or three points to the octane number of premium unleaded. The second is to reduce the engine's octane appetite by using mechanical means, such as changing pistons, or by using thicker or multiple head gaskets.

For valve protection, the Corvette owner has the choice of either using an additive or of making engine modifications that eliminate the need for valve protection. Some people have salted away stocks of additives with genuine lead, but nonlead additives containing sodium compounds will handle the valve protection role. The mechanical solution is to change to Stellite valves and hardened seats, which are impervious to the higher operating temperatures of unleaded gasoline. This is how modern engines survive just fine without lead.

For an older street Corvette that is driven casually, do you need to worry about the effects of unleaded fuel on valves? Probably not. Kent

Above and page 119: Well, here's one example where lousy storage didn't ruin a Corvette's value. This is the earliest Corvette known to exist, the third one built, as it appeared prior to its sale at the Rick Cole Auction Company's classic car auction held at Monterey, California, on August 21, 1987. Corvette enthusiasts Les Bieri, Howard Kirsch, and John Amgwert paid $37,000 plus commission. Not a small amount, to be sure, but less than one would expect for such a special Corvette. It wasn't the condition that drove the price down, but uncertainty about the car's authenticity. For one thing, it didn't have the correct frame. But in time, old GM records were located that documented the car's history. Seems that after 5,000 miles on GM's famed Belgian Block torture test, the car was reconditioned—including new frame—for retail sale, something that does not happen today because of liability reasons. 003 has been meticulously restored to its original factory-build condition and surely is one of the most special Corvettes in existence.

Left: As of January 1, 1996, the addition of tetraethyl lead to gasoline for automotive use was banned in all fifty states. The problems this poses for owners of 1971 and older Corvettes have to do with octane and valve seat lubrication. Moroso Octane Booster raises octane by two or three points when added to unleaded premium. Turner Laboratories Lead Substitute lubricates valve seats. Neither of these products contains tetraethyl lead.

Brooks, a friend with excellent engineering credentials, maintains that the whole issue of lead being necessary for valve protection in street cars is bunk. And he's felt that way for years. His first car was a brand-new '64 Corvette Spider. Because unleaded fuel burns so much cleaner, he ran his Corvair exclusively on unleaded (available then from Amoco as "white" gas) for 150,000 miles with absolutely no problem. So while I would certainly spend the few extra bucks to replace valves and seats if in the process of an engine rebuild, I would not worry about unleaded fuel's effect on valves or seats otherwise. For the use most of us give our classic Corvettes, it will never be a problem. Realize, however, that Corvettes exposed to high-performance demands like racing, autocross, and the like are a different story. Here, I would recommend preemptive mechanical work or, at a minimum, valve lubricating additives.

The previous discussion specified "automotive" pump fuel because another solution to both octane and valve seat wear is the use of aviation fuel. At this writing, high-octane leaded aviation fuel (tinted blue) is available. There is a legal issue because aviation fuel is not taxed for automotive use, so some airports will refuse to pump it into an automobile tank. I've pumped it myself into 5-gallon cans at small airports with no grief. Because aviation gas has a lower vapor pressure than auto gas, it can cause an automobile engine to be more difficult to start. However, if you blend one-fourth aviation gas with three-fourths premium unleaded auto gas, you'll get a terrific blend that will satisfy the octane appetite of stock 11:1 compression-ratio Corvette engines, will protect valve seats, and will not appreciably affect starting.

Oil

Have you ever been told that oil never wears out, it just gets contaminated? I've heard that for years, and it reminds me of the best mechanic I ever knew, Bob Burdette. Bob was a young ace at our local Studebaker dealership. When Studebaker went belly-up, he built a garage next to his house and went into business for himself. What made Bob such a good mechanic (and so entertaining) was that he didn't simply fix things, he analyzed them. He'd hold up something that had failed and say, "Now if the engineers had just included a gusset right here..." Back in the late 1960s, Bob became intrigued with an aftermarket product called the Franz Oil Filter. It didn't replace the existing filter; it was an *extra* filter. You'd mount this thing on the firewall or inner fender well. The sales pitch was that since oil never wore out, you'd never have to change oil (or conventional filter) again because the Franz would keep the oil clean. If that didn't get your attention, the filtering element would. It was a roll of toilet paper! Not the soft, expensive, perfumy variety. With the Franz, you wanted the hardest, cheapest, most tightly packed, least feminine-friendly rolls you could find. At the time, they cost a dime. The procedure was to change the element every 1,000 miles and add just enough oil to replenish what was dumped with the old roll.

Friends, this thing worked, at least visually. I put one on my '66 Corvette. Hedging my bets, I still changed oil and conventional filter, and when I did, the old oil came out looking like it was right out of the can. And it was always clean on the stick. Bob felt so strongly about this product that he closed up shop, bought a new Suburban, installed a Franz, welded the oil drain plug shut, and hit the road selling Franz Oil Filters. For reasons unrelated to the effectiveness of the product, the company failed. A descendant company, the Harvard Corporation, took the Franz's basic technology in a different direction. Harvard developed larger versions of the Franz filter design and went after commercial markets, especially really tough filtering environments like mining equipment. The company did so very successfully. When Bob retired, he was Harvard's Director of Technical Services.

There are oil lessons here that are relevant to a Corvette owner today. While oil itself never wears out, additives do. For example, the multiviscosity additives that make 10W30 oil act like 30W when hot and 10W when cold start to lose effectiveness at around 3,000 miles of normal driving. The 3,000-mile oil change recommendation of the quick-change places may strike some as excessively cautious, but there is some logic to it. Mechanic Bob ran that Suburban several hundred thousand miles without changing oil and without an engine rebuild, but he had to use straight-weight oil. As winter approached, he'd start adding 10-weight with toilet paper filter changes to thin the crankcase down; he'd do the opposite as warm weather loomed. This was too much hassle for me and why I looked at the Franz as a way to simply keep oil spotlessly clean between regular changes. And just because the oil was visibly clean, did it really retain all its lubricating efficiency? I doubted it, because there are acids and other contaminants that build up, so I wasn't going to risk my Corvette's engine to prove the point.

Still, mechanic Bob and my own engine-teardown experience combined to make me sensitive and keenly interested in oil issues. That's why, in writing updates for the 1992 *Corvette Black Book*, I was intrigued by Chevrolet's change to Mobil 1 synthetic oil as factory fill for Corvettes and the simultaneous elimination of engine oil coolers. Following up, I was told by Chevrolet engineers that Mobil 1 without an oil cooler held up and lubricated better than conventional oil with the cooler. That was

Oil never wears out but additives do.

Left: This Mobil 1 promotional piece coincided with the introduction of the 1997 Corvette, but Mobil 1 synthetic oil has been factory fill for Corvettes since 1992. Chevrolet engineers discovered that Mobil 1 lubricated a Corvette engine without an oil cooler better than conventional oil with an oil cooler. Synthetic oil has tremendous advantages over conventional, but that doesn't necessarily mean that everyone should start using it. For some engines, problems with oil consumption and leakage can be magnified.

an eye-opener. Mobil 1 has been factory-fill and recommended for Corvette engines since.

Synthetic's main advantage is resistance to thermal breakdown, but it also flows better at low temperatures. Synthetic oil has lower volatility, meaning it evaporates and boils away less than conventional oil. Synthetic resists oxidation and sludge buildup better, and it reduces friction compared with conventional. Use of synthetic for high-performance applications, for any 1992 or newer Corvette, and for any turbo application is a no-brainer. But what about older Corvettes?

When I became aware of the reasons for Corvette's change to synthetic oil in 1992, I immediately switched to synthetic for my 1967 Corvette with original miles still in the teens. A half-dollar-sized oil spot from the rear main seal suddenly grew to a foot-wide puddle. Synthetic's ability to get where conventional oil can't is a major lubricating advantage, but if you have any leaks, synthetic will magnify them. And while synthetic may evaporate and boil away less, if an engine is burning any conventional oil, it will burn more synthetic. Guaranteed.

Synthetic oil is fine for pre-1992 Corvettes that don't burn or leak oil. I'd certainly recommend its use after a complete rebuild of any Corvette

Above: Here's a simple but handy product for every do-it-yourselfer. These throwaway paper funnels are sold by Griot's Garage, a mail order auto parts company. Griot also sells a dispenser to hold the funnels, naturally.

They were prone to leakage around the piston seals.

engine. But I wouldn't recommend it for any Corvette that leaks or consumes oil. This doesn't mean you can't get some of synthetic's advantages. Because conventional and synthetic oils are completely compatible, you can blend. Most oil companies already sell blended products, but you'll do better if you blend yourself. Based on typical prices, you'd assume the prepackaged blends are about 25% synthetic, but experts tell me it's more like 10%, so they're a lousy value. I generally add 1 quart of synthetic to 4 quarts conventional in a typical 5-quart Chevy oil change. I've read that when blending, you should stick with the same brand. Synthetic formulations do vary by company, but how can they be evaluated? Since Chevrolet endorses Mobil, that's what I use.

One last thing. You may have heard that conventional oil should be used for new or rebuilt engines for several thousand miles because synthetic lubricates so effectively that it won't allow the engine to break in properly. The folks at Mobil tell me that's baloney. Synthetic is good, but it's not *that* good.

Brakes and brake fluid

The four-wheel disc brake system introduced on 1965 Corvettes (a delete-disc, credit option was available in 1965 only) and used through 1982 models cured one of the few shortcomings of Corvette performance. The problem was that the calipers of this braking system were prone to leakage around the piston seals. The piston material was anodized aluminum, and the calipers were either nodular cast iron or gray cast iron. If the anodizing came off the piston, there were electrolytic reactions between the iron and the aluminum. The real root of the problem, however, was that iron rusts.

What happened in the Corvette system was that as the brake pads wore, the pistons moved toward the rotors, taking up new positions in the bore of the iron caliper housings. Previously, this portion of the bore had not been protected from the elements, and the piston seal then stopped sealing as it came upon a corroded area. This wasn't a problem seen only in Corvettes driven in salty northern winters; nor was it restricted to high-mileage Corvettes.

The aftermarket introduction of brake calipers sleeved in stainless steel, combined with solid stainless-steel pistons, solved the problem and caliper cylinder wall corrosion became a thing of the past. Richter Systems, Dr. Vette, Vette Brakes, Muskegon Brake, and Stainless Steel Brake Corporation are companies whose sleeved caliper products I'm familiar with. I haven't had a bad experience with any, though my personal favorite is Richter Systems. You can exchange your Corvette's calipers for a sleeved set. Or if you want to retain your Corvette's actual calipers and don't mind the extra time required, you can have those sleeved. Other brake components, such as stainless-steel springs and levers for emergency brakes, also are available.

In this book's first edition, I wrote that a second major improvement for Corvette brakes was synthetic fluid. Synthetic does indeed have some remarkable properties and advantages, but I must now add some serious notes of caution.

Silicone brake fluid's big advantage is its incompatibility with water.

Conventional brake fluid absorbs moisture, which can lead to corrosion. Another nice silicone trait is that it won't hurt most finishes if accidentally spilled. Those of us who have dripped conventional brake fluid on a fender know what it can do.

Now to the drawbacks. Changing to silicone brake fluid isn't a matter of draining the old fluid and adding silicone. All the old fluid must be removed. *All* of it. Obviously, a good time to do this is when changing to sleeved calipers. Even then, I've heard stories about master cylinders that start leaking shortly after switching to silicone. Another problem develops with silicone fluid at higher elevations. At elevations over 5,000 feet, owners have reported a low, soft brake pedal with silicone fluid in Corvettes that were fine at normal elevations. It has to do with tiny traces of air in the brake system, amounts that apparently don't bother Corvettes with conventional fluid.

More ominously, I've been told of problems with silicone fluid experienced by some owners of older Corvettes after several years of use involving what appears to be incompatibility of silicone with certain types of seals. In some cases, seals swell. In others, seals deteriorate to a jelly-like consistency. These reports are anecdotal, though major manufacturers like Honda have switched back to conventional fluid after trying silicone. On the other hand, my own 1967 Corvette, which I sold two years ago, has had silicone fluid in it for over fifteen years without a problem.

To date, Corvettes have never come with silicone brake fluid as factory fill, and you should not change to silicone for any Corvette with ABS (1986 and later). Hib Halverson, writing in *Vette Magazine*, recommends

Do not change to silicone fluid for any Corvette with ABS.

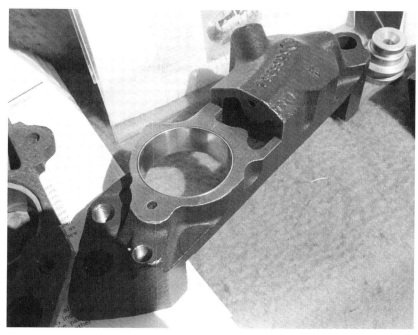

Page 124: It's a beautiful looking brake system, but 1965-1982 Corvette disc brakes were troublesome until the development of stainless steel bore sleeves.

Above: The Car Quest brake fluid is DOT 3, the standard grade of conventional fluid. The Valvoline brake fluid shown is synthetic. Don't confuse this with silicone. Valvoline's synthetic fluid replaces either DOT 3 or DOT 4 grades and is compatible with conventional fluid. It has the advantage of retaining less moisture.

Above right: This is a Richter Systems cutaway display of a sleeved caliper.

DOT 5.1-grade brake fluid, which has a higher boiling point than grades DOT 3 and 4, for ABS Corvettes used for racing or other high-performance applications.

So until I have more confidence in silicone, I'm sticking with conventional fluid regardless of Corvette model. Since the early sixties, Corvette braking systems have been sealed, so very little moisture gets in anyway. DOT 3-grade fluid is the standard, but you can upgrade to the more refined DOT 4, which I've done. If you stay with conventional fluid, you can minimize moisture accumulation damage by flushing the fluid periodically, especially if your Corvette is a classic with a breathing master cylinder cap. As a general guideline, I think fuild changes every one or two years, depending on the model year and use, are plenty adequate.

To reiterate my comments in the first chapter, most of the tips mentioned in this text are personal favorites of mine, the enthusiasts I consulted, or readers of this book's first edition who submitted their ideas. That certainly doesn't mean these are the only, or even the best, techniques. There is, after all, considerable variance in what different owners seek from their Corvettes. But the techniques do work—and work well. Perhaps by meshing them with your own time-proven tricks, you can make that special Corvette even more so.

Please write to me in care of Michael Bruce Associates, Post Office Box 396, Powell, Ohio 43065, to comment pro or con on anything in this text. I'd especially like to hear your detailing secrets so they can be included in a future edition of *Secrets of Corvette Detailing*.

Mike Antonick

Appendix

The following entries include sources and products mentioned in the text. Many other detailing sources and products are available.

Aircraft Spruce & Specialty
www.aircraft-spruce.com
Email: info@aircraft-spruce.com
Aircraft Spruce West
225 Airport Circle
Corona, CA 91720
800-824-1930
909-372-0555 (fax)
Aircraft Spruce East
900 S. Pine Hill Rd.
Griffin, GA 30223
800-831-2949
770-229-2329 (fax)

Castrol North America Automotive
Wayne, NJ 07474
800-642-0174

Calyx Corporation
P O Box 53277
Cincinnati, OH 45253
800-313-5671
513-923-1154 (fax)

Dave Cosner
316 Forestview Dr
Bedford, IN 47421

CRC Industries
Warminster, PA 18974
800-521-3168 (Technical)
800-272-8963 (Customer Service)

Dr. Vette
212 Seventh St SW
New Philadelphia, OH 44663
800-878-1022
www.drvette.com

DuPont de Nemours & Co. (Inc.)
Wilmington, DE 19898
800-441-7515

Eagle One Industries
Box 4246
Carlsbad, CA 92018
800-432-4531 (Customer Service)

Enviro-Tech International
Environmental Solutions
David & Shelley Salisbury
255 Metaire Lane
Madison, AL 35758
205-971-1457

GM Goodwrench
Dex-Cool Antifreeze
General Motors Corporation
Detroit, MI 48202

Griot's Garage
3500-A 20th St. E.
Tacoma, WA 98424
800-345-5789

Hot Stuff Manifold Dressing
Virginia Vettes
105 Lindrick Street
Williamsburg, VA 23188
757-229-0111 (orders)
757-565-1629 (fax)

IBIZ Inc.
750 East Sample Road
Pompano Beach, FL 33064
800-367-7929
305-783-7131 (fax)

Liquid Glass Enterprises, Inc.
P O Box 1170
Teaneck, NJ 07666
800-548-5307

Meguiar's Inc.
17991 Mitchell South
Irvine, CA 92614
714-752-8000
714-752-6659 (fax)
800-854-8073
800-347-5700 (care center)
www.meguiars.com

Micromesh
Wilton, IA
800-225-3006
www.micro-surface.com

Mobil
800-ASK-MOBIL (Mobil 1)
800-662-4525 (Gen. Tech Info)

Moroso Performance Products
80 Carter Drive
Guilford, CT 06437
800-544-8894

Muskegon Brake
848 E. Broadway
Muskegon, MI 49444
616-733-0874 (orders/tech)
616-733-0635 (fax)

Novus Inc.
Minneapolis, MN 55438
800-548-6872 (Nearest Distributor)

OEM Glass
P O Box 362
Bloomington, IL 61702
800-283-2122

Pine Ridge Enterprise
OmniBag, CarJacket
13165 Center Rd
Bath, MI 48808
800-5-CARBAG
www.carbag.com

PPG Industries Inc.
PPG Finishes
19699 Progress Drive
Strongsville, OH 44136

Prestone Products Corporation
Allied Signal
Danbury, CT 06810-5109
800-862-7737

R & G Enterprises
P O Box 1124
Exton, PA 19341
610-363-1547

Rain-X
Unelko Corporation
Scottsdale, AZ 85260
800-542-6424

Resolve
Reckitt & Colman Inc.
Wayne, NJ 07474-0945
800-228-4722

Red Line Synthetic Oil Corp.
6100 Egret Court
Benicia, CA 94510
707-745-6100

Restoration Battery
3335 Robinet Dr.
Cincinnati, OH 45238
513-451-1038

Richter Systems
2161 Goshen Hill Road
New Philadelphia, PH 44663
330-339-6054

Sid Savage Auto Dealer Supply, Inc.
27165 Northline Rd.
Taylor, MI 48180
800-521-1712

Spartan Chemical Company Inc.
110 N. Westwood Avenue
Toledo, OH 43607
800-537-8990

SS Brake Corp
Stainless Steel Brakes
11470 Main Rd.
Clarence, NY 14031
800-448-7722
716-759-8688 (fax)

Sta-bil Fuel Stabilizer
Gold Eagle Company
Chicago, IL 60632
800-367-3245

Stoner
1070 Robert Fulton Highway
P O Box 65
Quarryville, PA 17566
888-786-6373
717-786-0804
www.stonersolutions.com

Survival Air Systems
SAS Safety Corp.
Signal Hill, CA 90806

3M Automotive Trades Division
3M Center, Building 223-6N-01
St. Paul, MN 55144-1000
800-414-4000 (Car Questions)

Turner Laboratories Corporation
Danville, IL 61832

Turtle Wax, Inc.
P O Box 547
Bedford Park, IL 60499
www.turtlewax.com

Ultra Finish Products
Westwood, NJ 07675
800-666-8587

Valvoline Company
Division of Ashland, Inc.
Lexington, KY 40509
800-TEAM-VAL
http://www.valvoline.com

Vette Brakes
7490 30th ave N
St. Petersburg, FL 33710
800-237-9991
www.vettebrakes.com

VHT:PJH Brands
Scottsdale, AZ 85258-3328

Winners Circle International
7148 Stacy Lane
Chesterland, OH 44026
404-729-6347

Zymöl Enterprises, Inc.
P O Box 594
Chicago, IL 60499
800-999-5563 (voice)
203-483-0383 (tech assistance)
800-257-5050 (fax)
http://www.zymol.com

Note: Carbo Chlor, Casite, Dawn, DeMoist, Dow Scrubbing Bubbles, Endust, Gunk, G96, Marvel Mystery Oil, Minwax, Mother's products, Murphy Oil Soap, Pledge, Resolve, Simple Green, Soft Scrub, SOS, Trewax, WD 40, Woolite, and ZAR are common products available in hardware stores, grocery stores, drug stores, discount department stores, automobile stores, and other common outlets.

Corvette & Camaro Literature

Additional copies of *Secrets of Corvette Detailing, Second Edition*, are available directly from the publisher, Michael Bruce Associates, Inc., at $19.95 per copy. The following Corvette and Camaro books are also available directly from Michael Bruce Associates Inc. To order, enclose check or money order along with a brief description of the books you want. Add $3 shipping for each order (no quantity limit) shipped to the same address. All books are shipped in rigid containers, not in padded bags. Satisfaction is guaranteed unconditionally. Wholesale discounts are available for quantities of ten books or more. Please write for details:

Michael Bruce Associates, Inc.
PO Box 396
Powell, Ohio 43065

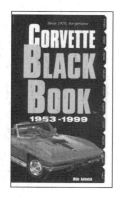

New editions of the *Corvette Black Book*, first published in 1978, are released annually. This pocket-sized marvel covers 1953 through the current models (the most current edition is always sent) and contains thousands of facts including options and option codes, exterior and interior colors and codes, production figures, serial numbers for body, engine, and component parts, and a compilation of the little details that make each Corvette model unique.

The *Black Book* also has a glossary of Corvette terms, a historical chronology and exterior color quantities for nearly all years. This is the book you see referred to in all the magazines, and the one poking out of astute Corvette enthusiasts' back pockets at shows around the world. Soft cover, 128 pages, 52 photos, uncountable facts. $12.95

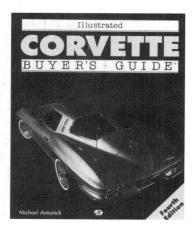

Written by Mike Antonick (author of the *Corvette Black Book*) and published by MBI Publishing, this fourth edition of the *Illustrated Corvette Buyer's Guide* includes all models from 1953 to 1997. This is considered the standard reference work for anyone interested in purchasing a Corvette. Each model's heritage, its strong and weak points, and what each is like to drive and own is described.

There's an exclusive five-star rating system for best buys, typical mechanical bugs, even cautions for the dreaded "bogus" Corvette. Bet of all, the "numbers match" terminology one sees in every Corvette ad is fully explained.

The *Corvette Buyer's Guide* is a must for anyone planning a Corvette purchase, but even the most astute enthusiast will love this tour through the evolution of a modern icon. Soft cover, 176 pages, 230+ photos, 7.5"x9.25," $17.95.

This is the companion to the famous *Corvette Black Book*. Now Camaro lovers can have their own pocket bible of Camaro facts. Introduced in 1985, completely rewritten and resized in 1993, and revised again for 1997, this new edition covers 1967-1997 models. It lists facts, numbers, codes, and the complete option scoop. For Camaros, options can be the difference between collectible and ho-hum. This book presents options in a comprehensive, yet easy to locate, year-by-year format.

The *Camaro White Book* also tells you how many of each Camaro factory option Chevrolet sold each year so you can determine what is really rare and what isn't. Not the old incomplete, inaccurate data charts you've seen reprinted elsewhere, this book is start-from-scratch, thoroughly researched and beautifully printed. Soft cover, 128 pages, 40 photos, $12.95.